GIFTS FROM THE HEART

NO

M

GIFTS FROM THE HEART

Editors of North Light Books

NORTH LIGHT BOOKS
CINCINNATI, OHIO
www.artistsnetwork.com

Gifts From the Heart. Copyright © 2004 by North Light Books. Manufactured in China. All rights reserved. The patterns and drawings in the book are for personal use of reader. By permission of the author and publisher, they may be either hand-traced or photocopied to make single copies, but under no circumstances may they be resold or republished. It is permissible for the purchaser to make the projects contained herein and sell them at fairs, bazaars and craft shows. No other part of this book may be reproduced in any form or by any electronic or mechanical means including information storage and retrieval systems without permission in writing from the publisher, except by a reviewer, who may quote a brief passage in review. Published by North Light Books, an imprint of F+W Publications, Inc., 4700 East Galbraith Road, Cincinnati, Ohio 45236. (800) 289-0963. First edition.

08 07 06 05 04   5 4 3 2 1

Library of Congress Cataloging-in-Publication Data

Gifts from the Heart : 60 gifts you can make in an hour or less / by the Editors at North Light Books.

p. cm.

Includes index.

ISBN 1-58180-576-4

1. Handicraft--Juvenile literature. I. North Light Books (Firm)

TT160.G433 2004

745.5--dc22

2004041544

Editors: Tricia Waddell and David Oeters

Designers: Stephanie Strang and Karla Baker

Layout Artist: Karla Baker

Production Coordinator: Sara Dumford

Photographers: Al Parrish, Brenda T. Martinez and Ken Trujillo

Photo Stylists: Mary Barnes Clark and Sylvie Abecassis

Metric Conversion Chart

to convert	to	multiply by
Inches	Centimeters	2.54
Centimeters	Inches	0.4
Feet	Centimeters	30.5
Centimeters	Feet	0.03
Yards	Meters	0.9
Meters	Yards	1.1
Sq. Inches	Sq. Centimeters	6.45
Sq. Centimeters	Sq. Inches	0.16
Sq. Feet	Sq. Meters	0.09
Sq. Meters	Sq. Feet	10.8
Sq. Yards	Sq. Meters	0.8
Sq. Meters	Sq. Yards	1.2
Pounds	Kilograms	0.45
Kilograms	Pounds	2.2
Ounces	Grams	28.4
Grams	Ounces	0.04

ABOUT THE DESIGNERS

Drenda Barker

Drenda Barker is a paper artist and has played with paper for over 20 years. She enjoys creating practical, yet fun, projects using all types of paper. Drenda has taught paper arts classes to both children and adults, and her work has been published in Somerset Studio magazine.

Debba Haupert

Debba Haupert and her company BoBella Craft Marketing & Design (www.bobella.com) provide marketing and design support for the craft and hobby industry. She provides new product development, marketing, sales, kit and package design/sourcing, trade show support, media and designer relations and craft design. Debba has been published in various books and magazines. She has demonstrated for craft manufacturers through appearances on The Carol Duvall show on HGTV, A.C. Moore videos and QVC.

Barbara Matthiessen

Barbara Matthiessen's design work covers a wide range of styles and mediums. She has written 43 craft booklets, contributed to nineteen multi-artist books and has created countless designs for magazines. While continuing to design for publication, she also develops kits, project sheets and sales models for manufacturers and is a contributing author for the book Collage Creations (North Light Books, 2004).

Mary Lynn Maloney

Mary Lynn Maloney is a craft designer and workshop teacher with a passion for creativity. After 12 years as a graphic designer, she fled the computer screen and got back to creating art with her hands. She loves history, art and travel, and these interests often influence her finished designs, giving her pieces a sense of another place or time.

TABLE OF CONTENTS

Introduction, 8

Gifts Between Friends, 10

Jacob's Ladder Stationery Set, 12

Tag Journal, 14

Mini Book Pendant, 15

Accordion Fold CD Holder, 16

Garden Journal, 18

Patterned Pencil Set, 19

Magnets in a Pillow Box, 20

Florentine Pushpin Set, 21

Collapsible Photo Album, 22

Blooming Pens, 24

Pretty Pushpin Holder, 25

Notecard Portfolio Set, 26

Gifts For All Occasions, 28

Plaster Word Plaques, 30

Shrink Art Plant Pokes, 31

Tri-Fold Mesh Frame, 32

Heart Pins, 33

Message in a Bottle, 34

Embossed Bookmarks, 35

Metallic Candle, 36

Heart Candle Snuffer, 37

Incense Burner Gift Set, 38

Bejeweled Photo Frame, 40

Domino Photo Holder, 41

Prayer Box Necklace, 42

Heart Brooch, 43

Love Bookmark, 44

Dog Tag Domino Pendant, 45

Baby Memory Book Cover, 46

Vintage Suitcase Photo Album, 47

Heart Cork, 48

Beaded Wine Charms, 49

Gift Cards and Packages, 66

Dress Up Card, 68

Purse Card, 70

Money Frame Card, 71

Butterfly Card, 72

Mesh Star Card, 72

Star Envelope Card, 74

Chinese Coin Card, 74

Matchbox Card, 76

Pillow Gift Box, 77

Fringe Benefits Card, 78

Money Fortune Cookie, 79

Embellished Bottles, 80

Vellum Sachets, 81

Chinese Take-out Box, 82

Happy Birthday Box, 84

Tag Box, 86

Templates, 88
Resources, 92
Glossary, 94
Index, 95

Gifts For the Home, 50

Lavender Banner, 52

Mosaic Candleholder, 53

Square Flowerpots, 54

Flower Frame, 55

All Keyed Up Box, 56

French Bulletin Board, 58

Vintage Correspondence Tray, 59

Collage Clock, 60

Dream Pillow, 61

Wind Chime, 62

Sun Catcher, 64

Sparkle Night-light, 65

GIFTS FROM THE HEART

A gift can be something heartfelt and meaningful. It can tell the story of the people who have found their way into your life and heart. It should speak of hugs, handshakes, laughter, time spent together and cherished memories. A gift can speak of friendship and brighten someone's day.

These pages are filled with gift ideas to help you celebrate the relationships you cherish. There is a garden journal made with pressed flowers, leaves and textured fibers. Its pages are waiting to be filled with photos and keepsakes. You'll find ideas to create personalized wine charms as a delightful favor for your next get-together. Or how would your best friend like a bejeweled photo frame made with a piece of memorabilia that not only holds a picture but becomes a part of the gift as well?

Not only will you find gift ideas, but ideas for gift presentation as well. The package can be as beautiful and meaningful as the gift itself. Create a couture dress card, or create a card decorated with a gorgeous beaded butterfly. Imagine giving a gift in an elegant vellum sachet, or a pillow box made of stunning textured paper.

Many of these projects are designed to be made in just a few minutes. They are crafted with materials you can find around the house. The projects are presented with simple step-by-step instructions that take the guesswork out of crafting and make it a delight. The introductions to the projects offer helpful gift ideas, so simply browsing the pages is an inspirational journey. The projects are filled with tips that give insight to the crafting techniques, honing your skills so you can get more from the time you spend crafting. At the end of many projects you'll find variation ideas. Every page is packed with ideas waiting to be discovered.

Show someone you care! Turn the pages of this book and begin crafting for everyone on your gift list. Never let another opportunity pass to tell someone how much they mean to you.

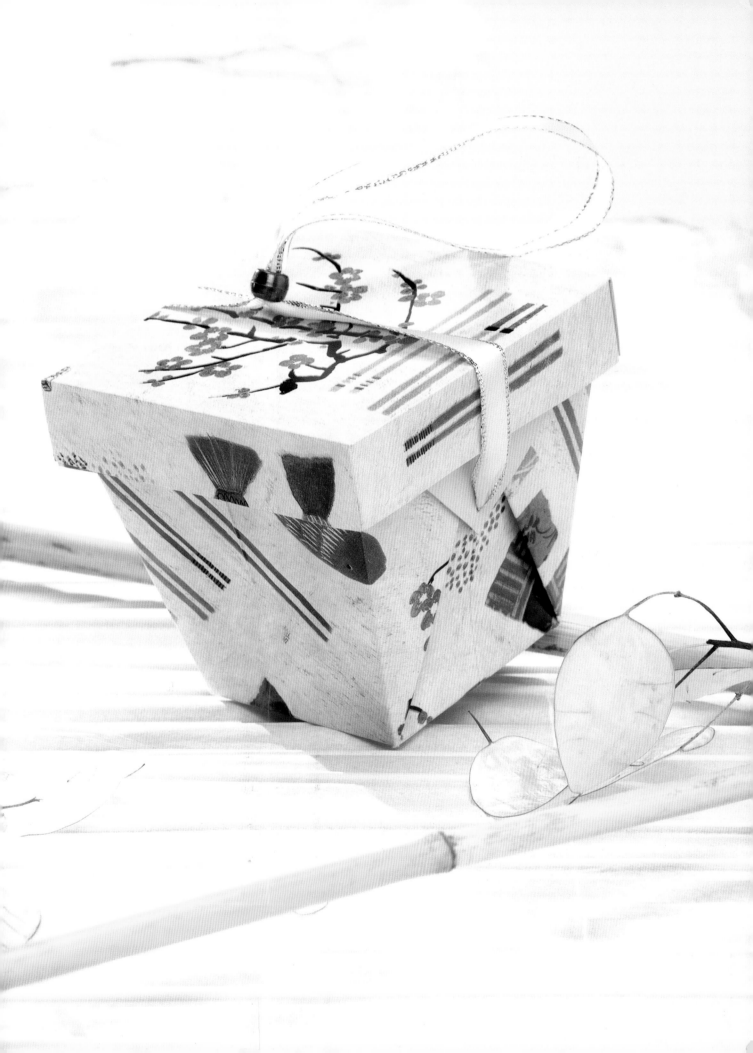

GIFTS BETWEEN FRIENDS

FRIENDS ARE THOSE PEOPLE WHO KNOW YOU BETTER THAN YOU KNOW YOURSELF. They are the ones you call to share in your successes, or when you need a helping hand and encouragement. Between friends is a long history of laughter, tears and adventure. When you gather together with friends, you dust off old memories and pass them around, perusing the past and letting joy fill up the moments. Then new memories are made for the next time you meet.

This next section is filled with gifts that would be perfect for friends that make life special. There is a mini book pendant that is sure to bring a smile to the face of a someone you hold dear. It is waiting to be filled with inspirational sayings and wishes. You'll find a stunning notecard portfolio set that will inspire anyone to write handmade cards. There is a gorgeous pencil set dressed in decorative paper that would be perfect for writing those letters.

Set aside a few moments in a quiet space, gather together some crafting supplies and give someone a gift that truly speaks of the friendship you share.

Remember the classic wooden Jacob's Ladder toy? This stationery holder was created with that toy in mind. The holder opens from either side, and you can flip it over and over in the same direction. This project is fun for all ages.

JACOB'S LADDER
STATIONERY SET

MATERIALS

- ♥ Four pieces chipboard, 4¾" × 6¼" (12cm × 16cm)
- ♥ Four pieces decorative paper, about 6" × 7½" (15cm × 19cm)
- ♥ Personalized stationery
- ♥ Three pieces of thin ribbon, ⅝" (2cm) wide, and 12" (30cm) long
- ♥ Double stick tape
- ♥ Glue stick
- ♥ Rubber band

1 Use the glue stick to cover all four pieces of chipboard with the decorative paper. Miter the corners of the paper. By placing the undecorated backs of the boards together, two boards (one set) will form the front cover, and the other two boards will form the back cover.

2 Lay one set of covered boards side by side in front of you, with the short sides horizontal and the back facing up. These will be the front cover.

3 On the left side of the left board, mark 1" (3cm) from the top and 1" (3cm) from the bottom of the board. On the right side of the same board, mark 3¼" (8cm) from the bottom.

4 On the back of the board, run a line of double stick tape on the four edges. Place one end of a ribbon on the 3¼" (8cm) mark. The other end of the ribbon will attach to the back cover. Place the ends of the other two ribbons on the 1" (3cm) marks. The double stick tape should hold the ribbons in place.

5 Place the other board from the front cover on top of the first board, with the backs of the boards together. Line up all sides of the boards and press them together. The double stick tape will secure the boards. You now have a completed front cover.

6 Place the stationery you want to include on this cover. Put a loose rubber band on the stationery to hold it in place until the ribbon is secure. Place the two lengths of ribbon from the left side of the board over and across the stationery. Set this aside until step 9.

7 On one board from the other set, which will be the back cover, mark 1" (3cm) from the top and 1" (3cm) from the bottom on the right side of the board. This is where you will place the other end of the ribbon attached to the front cover.

8 Run a line of double stick tape completely around the edge of this board, as you did on the front cover.

9 Place this board, with the tape side up, to the right of the completed front cover, and on top of the two lengths of ribbon that are covering the stationery. Take the ends of these ribbons, pulling until taut (but not too tight) and attach them to the 1" (3cm) marks you just made on the right side of the board. The ribbon should wrap around the front of this board and attach to the tape on the back of the board on the right side. The middle ribbon will be attached to the remaining board.

10 Lay the last board on top of the one you just completed, with the back sides together, but do not press them firmly together yet. Lay the middle ribbon on top of both boards, and place the end of the middle ribbon between the boards on the right side. The tape already on the board should hold the ribbon in place.

11 Press the boards firmly together. You should be able to open this stationery set from either side, or keep flipping it over and over in the same direction.

MATERIALS

♥ Five 2½" × 5" (6cm × 13cm) manila tags

♥ One 1½" × 3" (4cm × 8cm) manila tag

♥ One key tag

♥ Floral background stamp (Repousse Background from All Night Media)

♥ Journaling stamp set (Journaling II-Zettiology)

♥ Brown and gold pigment inks (Coffee Bean from Tsukineko and Brilliance Galaxy Gold)

♥ Gold embossing powder

♥ 18" (46cm) leather lacing

♥ Brown ink pen

♥ Heat gun

♥ Hole punch

Project by *Barbara Matthiessen*

This pocket-size journal is perfect to carry along on outings and vacations or to use at events. How about making one of these for everyone attending a reunion? Those new to journaling will appreciate the size and stamped journal sections.

TAG JOURNAL

1 Stamp a floral background in brown ink on one side of two of the larger tags. Apply ink to the stamp; place the stamp on a flat surface with the ink side up, then press the tag down onto stamp. Set the ink with a heat gun.

2 Create a cover tag using one of the tags with a floral background. Punch a hole on the left side, then stamp journal images on the tag surface using gold ink. Sprinkle gold embossing powder over the stamped images then remove the excess powder. Heat the stamp with a heat gun until the embossing powder has melted and appears glossy.

3 Stamp journal images on the small manila tag and the key tag using brown ink. Set the ink with a heat gun.

4 Stack the five larger tags together to form a journal. Place the embossed floral background tag on the front and the other tag with a floral background on the back of this stack, with the floral backgrounds facing outward. On the front of the stack place the small manila tag and the key tag. Thread the leather lacing through tag holes and then tie it in a double knot. Tie a pen to the other end of the lacing.

MORE IDEAS

■ Stamp a travel-themed journal as a bon voyage gift. Make a page for every port of call or city on the tour.

■ Make journals for preteen sleepovers using "girl power" stamps.

MATERIALS

- ♥ Two 1¼" × 1½" (3cm × 4cm) pieces of chipboard
- ♥ Two 1¾" × 2" (4cm × 5cm) pieces decorative paper
- ♥ Ten 1⅛" × 1⅜" (3cm × 4cm) pieces bond paper
- ♥ 6" (15cm) length of 20-gauge wire
- ♥ 30" (76cm) length of cord or ribbon
- ♥ Small jump ring
- ♥ Pony bead
- ♥ Glue stick
- ♥ ¹⁄₁₆" (2mm) hole punch
- ♥ Needle-nose pliers
- ♥ Wooden BBQ skewer or similar item to set wire in spiral form

Project by *Drenda Barker*

This is a wonderful gift for young girls to write down their secrets. It also looks great on a scrapbook page and can be used for all your journaling. It fits perfectly in many of the gift boxes in this book!

MINI BOOK PENDANT

1 Use a glue stick to cover both sides of the chipboard with decorative paper.

2 Punch holes in the decorative paper and chipboard covers. Punch five holes, ¼" (6mm) apart and ⅛" (3mm) in from the edge, in each of the covers.

3 Choose a back cover. Center the stack of ten pages on the back cover. Make sure the edges of the cover and pages line up. Punch five holes in the pages using the holes in the cover as a guide.

4 Place the front cover on top of the stack of the journal pages.

5 Use needle-nose pliers to form a small spiral loop at the end of the wire. With the holes on the left, insert the other end of the wire through the back of the first hole. Place the BBQ skewer along the spine of the book and wrap the wire around the skewer. Continue going through the holes and wrapping the wire around the spine, until you come to the end of the book. Remove the skewer.

6 Form another small loop at the end of the wire to secure everything in place.

7 Turn the book so the wire is on the left. Attach a jump ring to the top loop in wire.

8 Thread one end of the cord through the jump ring, and then add a pony bead through both ends of the cord. Push the bead to the end of the cord. Tie one knot in the cord close to the jump ring, and another at the very end of the cord.

MORE IDEAS

- Instead of a cord, why not use a ribbon for this project? Add an embellishment or a charm to the cover to make your gift even more special.

This is a great way to use CD envelopes. Turn an accordion book into a place to store not only CDs, but other, small, flat items. Stamps and stickers would fit perfectly in the envelopes and help keep your crafting area neat.

ACCORDIAN FOLD
CD HOLDER

MATERIALS

- ♥ Two $5\frac{1}{8}$" × $5\frac{1}{4}$" (13cm × 13cm) pieces of chipboard
- ♥ Two 5" × 11" (13cm × 28cm) sheets of cardstock
- ♥ Two $6\frac{1}{8}$" × $6\frac{1}{4}$" (16cm × 16cm) pieces decorative paper
- ♥ Two sheets coordinating bond paper to use as end papers
- ♥ Nine CD envelopes
- ♥ 18" (46cm) gold elastic cording for closure
- ♥ $\frac{1}{8}$" (3mm) hole punch
- ♥ Glue stick
- ♥ 1" (3cm) wide ruler
- ♥ Bone folder, or a similar scoring tool

TO MAKE THE ACCORDION

The accordion is basically a row of pleats. The hardest part in making the accordion is keeping the pleats the same size. Fold lines facing down are called valleys and fold lines facing up are called mountains.

1 To create the pleats, lay a 5" × 11" (13cm × 28cm) piece of cardstock in front of you so that the long side is horizontal. Place the ruler on the left edge of the cardstock, then score and fold a line 1" (3cm) from the edge of the paper. Unfold. Score and fold another line 1" (3cm) from the first line you made, and then unfold. Repeat until you reach the end of the cardstock, and then repeat this process on the other 5" × 11" (13cm × 28cm) piece of cardstock.

2 Attach the two pieces of cardstock together. Use glue stick to attach the last pleat of the cardstock pieces. Match up the cardstock ends so the connecting pleat is 1" (3cm) and there is not a break in the accordion fold. Trim the ends to make sure the pleats are all 1" (3cm).

3 After you attach the second cardstock, create the pleats of the accordion by folding in one direction, then the other, on all the fold lines. You should now have one continuous accordion with ten valley folds and nine mountain folds.

TO MAKE THE HOLDER

1 Cover one side of each piece of chipboard with decorative paper, mitering the corners and trimming as needed, to make the front and back covers.

2 Place one chipboard cover in front of you with the decorated side down. Make sure the $5\frac{1}{8}$" (13cm) side is horizontal.

3 Use double stick tape to attach the first pleat of the accordion folded cardstock flush to the right side of the decorated chipboard cover. The accordion will be smaller than the cover, so make sure the accordion paper is centered on the cover.

4 Place the other cover in front of you, decorated side down and the $5\frac{1}{8}$" (13cm) side horizontal. Use double stick tape to attach the last pleat to the left side of this cover.

5 Glue the bond paper to the inside covers. The bond papers should be placed directly on top of the pleat, and butted up to the edge that is attached to the accordion fold. This will hide where the accordion folded paper is attached to the chipboard. Note that the size of the bond papers is smaller than the covers, so make sure to center the bond paper.

6 Place double stick tape on the bottom edge of the back of each envelope. The bottom of each envelope, with the opening to the right, should fall into each valley fold. Press the envelopes into place. Fill the entire book this way.

7 Punch two holes in the back cover for the elastic closure. The holes should be $1\frac{1}{2}$" (4cm) from the outside edge of the cover, and $\frac{1}{2}$" (1cm) from the right and the left edges of the cover.

8 Thread the elastic cording through the holes and tie a bow on top of the holder.

♥ 8½" × 5½" (22cm × 14cm) pre-purchased handmade paper scrapbook with a natural fiber cover

♥ ¼" (6mm) round white hang tag

♥ Assorted pressed flowers and leaves

♥ A yard (90cm) each of textured fibers, purple, blue and earth tones

♥ A yard (90cm) of ⅛" (3mm) silver metallic ribbon

♥ Small alphabet rubber stamp sets (PSX Designs)

♥ Archival dye inkpad in Burnt Sienna (ColorBox)

♥ ⅛" (32mm) hole punch

♥ Flower shaped eyelet

♥ Eyelet setter and hammer

♥ Metal edge ruler

♥ Small cutting board

♥ Craft knife

♥ Scissors

♥ Matte découpage adhesive

Project by *Mary Lynn Maloney*

This is a beautiful and useful book for anyone who keeps a garden. Use the pages to make sketches of possible landscaping layouts, to paste photos of interesting flowers and plants or to make notes of what worked (and what didn't!) from season to season. This book would be a great addition to a gift basket containing seed packets and small gardening tools.

GARDEN JOURNAL

1 Place the small cutting board between the scrapbook cover and the first page. Using a pencil and ruler, draw a rectangle measuring approximately 2" × 3¼" (5cm × 8cm) on the bottom right-hand section of front cover. Carefully cut out the rectangle, leaving a window in front cover.

2 Trace the window opening lightly onto the first page of the book, then open the book. Using the pencil tracing as a guide, glue sprigs of pressed leaves at the top edge of the rectangle. Brush a small amount of matte adhesive over the pressed leaves. Use the Burnt Sienna ink and the alphabet set to stamp the word "garden" near bottom edge of rectangle. Erase any visible pencil lines.

3 Glue the pressed flowers and leaves onto the white hang tag. Brush over the hang tag with matte adhesive and let it dry.

4 Punch a hole in the center of the tag and insert the flower eyelet. Set the eyelet. Glue the knotted end of the assembled hang tag onto the page so that the tag will dangle down into window area.

5 Close the book. Cut a 12" (30cm) length of earth tone textured fiber and lightly glue it around the window opening on the book cover. Secure the pages of the scrapbook with textured fibers and metallic ribbon. Tie all fibers into a secure knot. Trim the excess fibers.

Project by *Mary Lynn Maloney*

Who said pencils had to be boring? The humble pencil is dressed in decorative wrappings and given an interesting and unexpected home in a glass test tube with a cork topper. This is an easy and unusual gift for someone who's hard to buy for.

PATTERNED PENCIL SET

1 Cut the decorative papers to 6" × 2" (15cm × 5cm).

2 Use a glue stick to generously cover the back of one piece of decorative paper. Wrap the paper around a pencil, trimming any excess and creating a neat seam. Press the paper with your fingers to smooth. Cover the remaining pencils with the other sheets of decorative papers and a glue stick.

Let them dry, then sharpen the pencils to a length to fit within the test tube.

3 Cut a 1" (3cm) circle from a scrap of decorative paper and glue it to one side of the white tag. Cut a ⅝" (2cm) square from another scrap of paper and glue it on top of the paper circle. Use the craft glue to glue a bead onto the center of the square. Let the glue dry.

4 Knot the textured fiber and the silver cord around the top edge of the cork. Secure the fibers with a dab of craft glue under the knot.

5 Thread three beads onto the string of the white tag. Loop and knot the opposite end of the string through the fibers tied around cork.

Project by *Mary Lynn Maloney*

Magnets

♥ 3⅛" × 2⅛" (8cm × 5cm) piece of cardstock

♥ Four clear, flat glass marbles

♥ Four ½" (1cm) diameter round magnets

♥ ½" × 3" (1cm × 8cm) magnetic strip

♥ Four computer-printed or handwritten words (length and size must fit under the marbles)

♥ Dimensional adhesive or tacky glue

♥ Double stick tape

♥ E6000

Pillow Box

♥ 5" × 7½" (13cm × 19cm) piece of cardstock

♥ 3¼" × 1½" (8cm × 4cm) piece of acetate

♥ Double stick tape

♥ Craft knife

♥ Cutting mat

These magnets serve as helpful reminders at home or at work and can be stored in this beautiful handcrafted box. This makes a nice bonus to add to the gift tag or card on another present.

MAGNETS IN A PILLOW BOX

TO MAKE THE MAGNETS

1 Put a small amount of dimensional adhesive or tacky glue over one of the words, then cover it immediately with a marble. Hold the marble in place until the glue begins to set. Repeat for the other words and marbles. Let them dry completely.

2 Place a small amount of E6000 on each of the round magnets and attach them to the marbles. Hold the marbles in place a few seconds until the glue begins to set. Let them dry completely.

3 Attach the magnetic strip to the center of the 3⅛" ×2⅛" (8cm × 5cm) piece of cardstock using double stick tape. Place the completed magnets on the magnetic strip.

TO MAKE THE PILLOW BOX

1 Use the template on page 88 to draw a box on the cardstock. Cut out the box shape, including the rectangle marked in the center.

2 Place a thin strip of double stick tape around the inside edge of the rectangle shape on the box. Center the acetate on top of the tape and press it in place.

3 Place a strip of double stick tape on a box edge that will be folded inside. Then fold one end of the box up and insert the magnets. Close the other end to seal.

- ♥ 8½" × 11" (22cm × 28cm) piece of ⅛" (.3cm) foamboard
- ♥ 5" × 7" (13cm × 18cm) piece of cork paper
- ♥ 5" × 7" (13cm × 18cm) piece of sage green handmade paper
- ♥ 4" × 5" (10cm × 13cm) piece of Florentine print decorative paper
- ♥ Four clear flat glass marbles
- ♥ Four clear plastic pushpins
- ♥ Celadon pigment ink (ColorBox)
- ♥ 3" × 5" (8cm × 13cm) drawstring millcloth bag
- ♥ ½" (1cm) decorative plastic button
- ♥ Matte découpage adhesive
- ♥ Glass adhesive
- ♥ Fabric glue
- ♥ Glue stick
- ♥ Matte spray sealer
- ♥ Paintbrush
- ♥ Metal edge ruler
- ♥ Craft knife

Project by *Drenda Barker*

Packaging is the key to making a simple gift something special. An elegant set of push pins is arranged on a custom corkboard card, then slipped into a charming mesh bag. Change the look to suit the recipient by changing the paper used on the pins.

FLORENTINE PUSHPIN SET

1 Trace the flat back of the marbles onto the Florentine paper and cut out the tracings. Brush découpage adhesive onto the bottom of a marble and place it on the tracings. Brush another layer of the adhesive over the back of the paper. Repeat the process with all the marbles, then let them dry.

2 Place a dab of glass adhesive onto the head of the plastic pushpin and press the pin onto the back of a paper covered marble. Repeat this step with the rest of the pins and marbles.

3 Use a ruler and a craft knife to cut a 2⅜" × 4⅜" (6cm × 11cm) piece of foamboard. Cover the foamboard with the sage paper using a glue stick, mitering the corners to reduce the bulk and trimming the paper as needed. Cover any exposed area on the back of the foamboard with leftover sage paper.

4 Cut a second piece of foamboard to 1⅝" × 3⅝" (4cm × 9cm). Cover this piece of foamboard with cork paper in the same manner as the step above. Glue the cork covered board onto the center of the sage paper covered board and let them dry.

Press the assembled pushpins into the corkboard.

5 Tap the Celadon ink onto the decorative button to give the button a patina effect. Spray the button with a matte spray sealer. Use fabric glue to adhere the button to the bottom right edge of the millcloth bag. Be careful not to glue the sides of the bag together.

MORE IDEAS

Check out the Pretty Push Pinholder on page 25 as a variation project.

One simple origami fold is used to create this fun album. Photos can be placed on both sides of the pages with lots of room left to journal. A pretty ribbon keeps everything secure.

COLLAPSIBLE PHOTO ALBUM

MATERIALS

- ♥ Two 4½" (11cm) square pieces of posterboard
- ♥ Two 5" (13cm) square pieces of decorative paper
- ♥ Five 8½" (22cm) square pieces of cardstock (three pieces should be of one color, and two pieces of another color)
- ♥ 25" (64cm) length of ½" (13mm) wide ribbon
- ♥ Jewel for the front of the album
- ♥ Glue Dot adhesive or multi-purpose adhesive, such as E6000
- ♥ Glue stick
- ♥ Double stick tape

1 Use a glue stick to cover both posterboard squares with decorative paper. Miter the corners and trim as necessary.

2 All of the pages in the photo album will be constructed the same way. The only difference is, when actually assembling the album, each page will be glued with the vertical fold line facing opposite directions. Take one piece of cardstock and fold it in half. Crease, unfold, then rotate the paper one-quarter turn and fold cardstock in half again. Crease and unfold.

3 Place the paper in front of you so it is in a diamond shape. Bring the bottom point up to the top point and fold. Crease the cardstock on this fold.

4 With the paper still folded in half diagonally, hold the paper in your left hand, with your thumb just to the left of the center point. With your right hand, push up on the bottom right fold, close to the point. Viewed from the side, you should see a square with a vertical line through it. Push on this vertical line and crease it. You should now have two points on the right side. Repeat this for the left side of the cardstock.

5 Repeat steps 2 through 4 for all five pieces of cardstock. When finished, place them unfolded in front of you.

6 (See the illustration below.) Each piece of cardstock will be glued to the bottom square of another piece of cardstock. Start with the first color. Place one sheet on your work surface with the vertical fold line facing toward you. Next, take a sheet of the second color cardstock. Turn it over and glue it on top of the bottom square of the first color. You should now have a vertical line facing up on the first cardstock and a vertical line facing down on the second cardstock.

7 Turn the entire project over. Glue another sheet of cardstock from the first color on top of the bottom square of second color, with the vertical fold line facing up. Repeat this process two more times so that you

end with the first color. This is your album. Refold the album on the existing fold lines. All of the pages should fold onto each other, and you should end up with a stack that is 4¼" (11cm) square.

8 Place one cover in front of you with the decorated side facing down. This will be the back cover. Place a piece of double stick tape in the middle of the left and right edges of the cover. Place the length of ribbon in the center of the cover and secure it to the tape on the edges.

9 Run a line of double stick tape around the edge of the cardstock. Place the album in the center of the back cover, on top of the ribbon, and press it into place. Then run a line of double stick tape around the top of the cardstock album. Place the front cover in the center of the album and press it into place.

10 Tie a bow with the ribbon to secure the album in place. Use a Glue Dot or E6000 to secure a jewel or embellishment to the front of the album. Pictures can be glued on the full pages in the album, with journal and caption notes written on the folded pages.

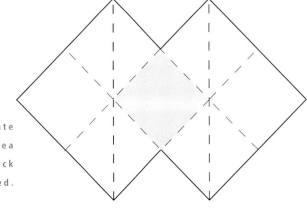

Dotted lines indicate folds. The shaded area is where the cardstock squares are attached.

Project by Brenda Barker

Project by Debba Haupert

MATERIALS

- ♥ Three ball point pens
- ♥ Floral tape
- ♥ Silk flower blooms and leaves
- ♥ Glass flower pot (optional)
- ♥ Black glass marbles (optional)
- ♥ Wire cutter
- ♥ Wire pliers
- ♥ Packing tape (or duct tape)

Part functional and part floral, these pen plants are a beautiful way to take a message or write a thank you note. Create a bouquet of blooming pens in their own glass flower pot. No green thumb required, these blooming pens will brighten any room with blossoms year-round.

BLOOMING PENS

1 Using a wire cutter, clip the stem of a silk flower 1" (3cm) below the bloom. Curl the end of the stem below the bloom with wire pliers to form a circle to fit around the pen.

2 Slip the flower stem onto the pen and hold the bloom in place with a 2" to 3" (5cm to 8cm) piece of packing or duct tape.

3 Begin wrapping floral tape around the base of the pen. Continue wrapping to the top of the pen near the bloom. Then wrap the tape back down the pen. Add leaves under the edge of the tape. Tear the tape at the bottom of the pen.

4 Repeat steps 1 through 3 to make a bouquet of floral pens.

5 For a fun gift presentation, fill a glass flower pot with black glass marbles to hold the pens.

MORE IDEAS

- Hot glue a silk bloom to the cover of an address book or memo paper holder for a matching set.
- Create a fun gift presentation by wrapping tissue paper around the pot (tied with bright ribbon). Leave the blooms exposed like a lovely bouquet!
- Tell your friend to just remove and replace the ink cartridge when it runs out to continue using these blooming pens for many, many seasons.

Project by *Drenda Barker*

MATERIALS

♥ 2" × 2" (5cm × 5cm) piece of foam core

♥ 3" × 3" (8cm × 8cm) piece of decorative paper

♥ 3¼" × 5¼" (8cm × 13cm) folded piece of a file folder

♥ 3" × 3" (8cm × 8cm) piece of acetate

♥ Four clear, flat glass marbles

♥ Four thumbtacks

♥ Small pictures (for under the marbles)

♥ Thread, cord or yarn for handle

♥ Computer-printed label

♥ ⅛" (3mm) hole punch

♥ Hook and loop fastener

♥ Double stick tape

♥ Dimensional adhesive

♥ E6000

♥ Ruler

♥ Craft knife and cutting mat

This is a fun and easy gift that your friends will love. Using a colored file folder to construct the holder will allow you to coordinate colors. It makes a great decorative accent for any office.

PRETTY PUSHPIN HOLDER

1 Place a small amount of dimensional adhesive on top of a picture, and then immediately place a flat marble over the picture. Before the glue sets, clean up any glue from around the marble.

2 Before the glue has dried completely, cut away the excess paper and attach the marble to the thumbtack using E6000 or extra strength adhesive. Do this for all the marbles and pictures

3 From the bottom edge of a closed file folder, measure and cut a piece that is 3¼" (8cm) wide and 5¾" (15cm) tall. Cut through both the front and back of the file folder.

4 File folders usually come pre-scored at the bottom. To make the project more narrow, fold and crease to leave a ½" (13mm) fold at the bottom of the holder. This fold line will become the bottom edge of the front of the holder. Unfold.

5 The front of the holder is only 4¼" (11cm) long. Measure from the bottom edge you just made and cut off the excess top of the file folder.

6 Cut a 2¼" (6cm) square opening ½" (13mm) up from the bottom edge of the holder. Inside the holder use double stick tape to attach acetate over the opening you just made.

7 From the back of the holder, score and crease a fold 1" (3cm) from the top. On this same fold line, measure ¾" (19mm)

from both the right and left sides and make a small pencil mark. Use your ⅛" (3mm) hole punch to punch holes on these marks.

8 Thread the material for the handle through the holes and tie a knot inside of the holder to secure the handle. With both halves of the hook and loop fastener still together, attach one side to the center of the 1" (3cm) fold. Close the front of the holder and secure the other half of the fastener.

9 Cover the foam core with decorative paper. Use double stick tape to attach the foam core to the holder ¾" (19mm) from the bottom fold. You should be able to see the decorated foam core through the window of the holder. If you would like, use your computer to create a label for the gift.

This gift just might tempt its recipient to log out of E-mail and spend some time writing an old-fashioned letter. When the notecards are all gone, the portfolio can hold photos, letters, postcards, mementos or journal scribblings.

NOTECARD PORTFOLIO SET

MATERIALS

- ♥ Large sheet of 140# cold-press watercolor paper
- ♥ Set of five notecards and envelopes
- ♥ 5" × 7" (13cm × 18cm) piece of decorative green speckle paper
- ♥ 5" × 7" (13cm × 18cm) piece of maroon marbled paper
- ♥ ³⁄₈" × 5¹⁄₂" (10mm × 14cm) strip of dark green corrugated cardstock
- ♥ Postmarked letter rubber stamp (Stampa Rosa)
- ♥ Face and clock collage rubber stamp (Acey Ducey)
- ♥ Vatican Wine chalk finish dye inkpad (Stampa Rosa)
- ♥ Copper pigment inkpad (Tsukineko)
- ♥ Black archival dye inkpad (Memories)
- ♥ Two yards (2m) each of decorative textured fibers: green/grey and blue/green
- ♥ ³⁄₄" to 1" (10mm to 25mm) piece of blue seaglass, washed and dried
- ♥ Cup of hot tea
- ♥ Matte spray sealer
- ♥ Spray bottle
- ♥ Craft knife
- ♥ Glue stick
- ♥ Craft glue
- ♥ Gem-Tac

1 Pour a cup of strong tea into a spray bottle. Use the spray bottle to tea stain one side of a sheet of watercolor paper. Let the paper dry.

2 Trace the template shape, found on page 89, onto the tea-stained side of the watercolor paper. Cut and score the paper using the template as a guide. Lay the tea-stained side up with the largest flap on the left.

3 Use the Vatican Wine ink to randomly stamp the collage image onto the edges of the top, right and bottom flaps. Bleed the ink off the paper edges. Stamp one collage image on lower right side of front flap. Use the Copper ink to randomly stamp the letter image onto the right-hand flap, overlapping the collage image. Run the Copper inkpad along all outer edges of the flaps. Let the inks dry.

4 Tear one edge of the decorative green paper. Cut the decorative paper to form a wedge shape for the front flap. Use the front flap to guide your cut and leave the torn edge on the left-hand side. Tear the maroon marbled paper to fit behind the green paper with just a bit peeking out on the left edge. Layer and glue the papers together. Glue the assembled wedge to the front flap and trim any overhanging papers.

5 Stamp the collage image in Vatican Wine ink onto the lower right corner of all the notecards. Decorate the envelope flaps with swirls from the Vatican Wine and Copper inkpads. Use black archival ink to stamp letter images at an angle on the envelope backs. Let the stamped images dry. Stamp a portion of the letter stamp onto the seaglass using the Copper ink. Spray the seaglass with matte sealer.

6 Tear the dark green corrugated cardstock into five small pieces, each about ³⁄₈" (10mm) square. Use Gem-Tac to glue the pieces on top of each other like a sandwich. Edge the remaining piece of corrugated cardstock with the Copper inkpad. Glue the corrugated cardstock sandwich to the center of this piece of cardstock. Glue the assembled piece, sandwich facing up, at a slight angle onto the center of the green speckled paper on the front flap. Leave about a ³⁄₈" (10mm) overhanging edge of cardstock over the flap.

7 Use Gem-Tac to glue the stamped seaglass on top of the sandwich piece. This will raise seaglass to make room for the fiber closure. Let the Gem-Tac dry. Cut fibers 24" (61cm) long and carefully tie the fibers under the seaglass. Lightly knot them on the lower left side of the glass. The short end of the fibers should be about 3" (8cm) long.

8 Gather the notecards and envelopes into a bundle and wrap them with the remaining fibers, trimming the excess as desired. Place the notecard set in the portfolio and close the flaps. Wrap the long end of the fibers around the portfolio, then wrap it around the seaglass to close.

GIFTS FOR
ALL OCCASIONS

THERE ARE MANY REASONS TO GIVE GIFTS, but sometimes the sweetest and most heartfelt gifts are given for no reason at all. Do we really need a reason to tell someone we love how much they mean to us? This section is filled with projects to help you celebrate every special occasion and holiday, and every special moment in between. A browse through these pages will reveal treasures for even the most finicky of recipients, and may even guide your creative process in a direction you may not have first considered.

What about an inspirational message inscribed on a keepsake note you can wear in a necklace? How about a jeweled heart made with wire that is not only a gorgeous decoration, but a candle snuffer as well? It makes a perfect gift for a friend that loves candles. Is there a friend that would adore a memory book cover that takes just moments to make? Or how about a beautiful incense burner set that you can craft yourself in less than an afternoon?

These gifts are all inexpensive and easy to make. Before you spend another day shopping, sit down with this book and spend a few moments letting your mind go on a creative gift-giving journey.

MATERIALS

- ♥ 3" × 7¼" (8cm × 18cm) wood slat
- ♥ Dusty blue or green acrylic paint
- ♥ Glass beads and fibers to coordinate with paint
- ♥ 18" to 30" (46cm to 76cm) 18-gauge wire or sheer ribbon
- ♥ Word stencil
- ♥ Spackle (available at hardware stores for patching sheetrock walls)
- ♥ 1" (25mm) wide paintbrush
- ♥ Putty knife
- ♥ Drill with ¹⁄₁₆" (2mm) bit
- ♥ Scissors
- ♥ Paper towel
- ♥ Toothpick

Express a thought, idea or sentiment on a plaque to show you care. A slightly distressed paint finish teamed with glass beads and beautiful fibers makes these plaques a unique and inspirational gift.

PLASTER WORD PLAQUES

1 Drill holes in the upper right and left corners of the wood slat.

2 Spread a thin layer of spackle over the plaque using a putty knife. Center the word stencil on the slat and hold it down firmly while you spread more spackle over the stencil. Pull the stencil straight up and off the slat in one motion. Clean up any letter edges and open up drilled holes with a toothpick. Allow the spackle to dry.

3 Wet the paintbrush first, then brush paint across the plaque. Wipe off the excess paint with a paper towel. This will leave paint in the spackle recesses. Allow the slat to dry.

4 Run wire or ribbon from the back of the slat to the front through holes you drilled. Twist the wire into a spiral around itself, or tie knots in ribbon to secure it to the slat. Thread beads onto the ribbon or wire. Curl the wire between beads if desired. Secure the opposite side of the ribbon or wire when you are finished.

5 Gather three or four fibers together. Tie the fibers around one end of the ribbon or wire.

MORE IDEAS

- Make name plaques to hang on doors.
- Add one of these plaques to a spa gift basket containing lotion, soaps and bath sponges for an elegant gift.

♥ One sheet of opaque shrink plastic

♥ 7 grams white/crystal, green mix or blue mix E beads

♥ 18-gauge plastic coated silver wire

♥ 24-gauge wire

♥ Ultrafine point permanent black marker

♥ Colored pencils

♥ #400 grit sandpaper

♥ 1/8" (3mm) hole punch

♥ Scissors

♥ Heat gun or oven

♥ Mat board scrap or heavy cardboard for the oven

♥ Bamboo skewer

♥ Optional: Round-nose pliers

Project by *Drenda Barker*

Add a touch of whimsy to any potted plant or flower arrangement with fanciful bug plant pokes. This is a project children would love to help you create. Let them color the bugs.

SHRINK ART **PLANT POKES**

1 Lightly sand one side of the shrink plastic.

2 Place the plastic over the patterns on pages 89 and 90 and trace over the design lines using a black marker.

3 Use colored pencils to color the designs. Colors will intensify as plastic shrinks.

4 Cut out the patterns. Punch a hole near the top of the designs at least 1/8" (3mm) away from the cut edge.

5 Heat the plastic designs. To shrink, hold down the plastic with the blunt end of a skewer while heating the plastic with a heat gun. Make sure the gun is at least 2" (5cm) from the plastic. Turn the piece over and heat it from opposite side until the plastic lies flat. Or, to shrink it in an oven, set the oven to 225° F (105° C). Place the plastic on a mat board and set it in the center of the oven. The piece should shrink in 1-2 minutes.

6 Cut one 20" (51cm) piece of 18-gauge wire for each plant poke. Twist a spiral in one end of the wire. Slide the shrink art bug onto wire until it sits facing forward at the base of the spiral. About 1½" (4cm) below the spiral create a hook shape in the wire.

7 Thread beads onto a 22" (56cm) length of 24-gauge wire. Spiral wrap this wire four times tightly around the wire poke with the shrink plastic bug. Leave 1½" (4cm) of wire at the straight end and the spiral holding the shrink plastic bug free from the 24-gauge wire. Wrap the end of wire around the poke four times then trim off the excess wire.

8 Thread the remaining beads onto 12" to 18" (30cm to 46cm) of 24-gauge wire. Twist a spiral loop in each end of this wire, then randomly wrap the wire between the beads around a bamboo skewer to curl it. To attach this wire to the poke, wrap the middle of this beaded wire around the base of the spiral holding the shrink plastic bug.

TIP

The shrink plastic will twist and curl as it shrinks but will be flat when finished. Should your piece not be as flat as you would like, place it between the pages of a large book while it is still warm. Make sure you wear gloves when handling hot plastic.

♥ Six sheets of colored mesh origami papers: orange, purple, magenta, light blue, green, yellow

♥ Twelve gold ⅛" (3mm) eyelets

♥ Eyelet setting tool and hammer

♥ Two yards gold tapestry braid

♥ Large eye tapestry needle

♥ Hole punch

♥ Bone folder

Project by Debba Haupert

This fun frame is crafted with mesh origami paper and eyelets. The metallic thread stitches act as hinges to allow the frame to stand on its own in a zig-zag shape. The ease of popping photos in and out makes this a great gift for a friend who likes to display new photos of her kids or pets on a regular basis.

TRI-FOLD MESH FRAME

1 Put the purple origami sheet on top of the orange, the magenta origami sheet on top of the light blue, and the green origami sheet on top of the yellow. You now have three sets of combined papers.

2 Fold the corners of the orange/purple origami paper set inward so that all the points meet in center. Crease the folds with a bone folder. Repeat this step with all the sets of origami papers.

3 Keeping the folds you made in the last step, fold and crease all the original points of the orange/purple set outward so that points are now even with outer edge of the square.

4 Punch a hole near one corner through all the folds of origami paper. Insert and set an eyelet into the hole. Repeat this with all four points, so that you create a square window opening, and then repeat steps 3 and 4 with all sets of colored mesh papers.

5 Thread the tapestry needle with a length of the gold braid and knot the end. Choose an assembled mesh square as your center frame. Use a simple, loose whip-stitch to join this center square to the two remaining mesh squares on the right and left. Cut photos slightly larger than the opening and place them in the frame.

♥ 3" × 3" (8cm × 8cm) piece of chipboard

♥ Embossing stamp pad

♥ Extra thick embossing powders

♥ Rubber stamp (should not have fine detail)

♥ ¹⁄₁₆" (2mm) hole punch

♥ Jump ring

♥ Beads on a pin

♥ Gold paint pen

♥ Pin back

♥ Pliers

♥ Scissors

♥ Craft glue

♥ Heat gun

Project by *Drenda Barker*

Keep a few of these pins on hand for a quick gift. Use a different rubber stamp image to personalize each gift you make. Although perfect as a gift in itself, these pins would look just as lovely topping off a present.

HEART PINS

1 Trace the pattern on page 88 and cut out the heart shape from the chipboard.

2 Using the ¹⁄₁₆" (2mm) hole punch, punch a hole at the bottom tip of the heart. Be sure not to punch too close to the edge.

3 Ink a rubber stamp with embossing ink.

4 Press the heart-shaped chipboard into the embossing stamp pad. Sprinkle it with the extra thick embossing powder, and then shake off the excess powder.

5 Secure your heart on your work surface before you use the heat gun. Once secure, melt the embossing powder on the heart with the heat gun. When finished, press the heart into embossing ink again, then sprinkle it with more embossing powder. Repeat this process until you have about four layers of embossing powders melted on the chipboard heart.

6 After melting the final layer, remove the heart from the work surface. Impress the heart with the stamp while the embossing powder is still hot. Leave the stamp on the heart a few seconds to cool then remove the stamp.

7 Apply gold ink from a paint pen to the back of the heart.

8 Attach a jump ring to the bottom of the heart, then attach the beads on a pin to the jump ring. You may need pliers to attach the jump ring.

9 Attach the pin back with craft glue to the back of the heart.

TIP

To keep the heart secure while using the heat gun, use a small bit of reusable adhesive on the back of the heart and place it in a small mint tin. Be careful— the melted powders will be hot!

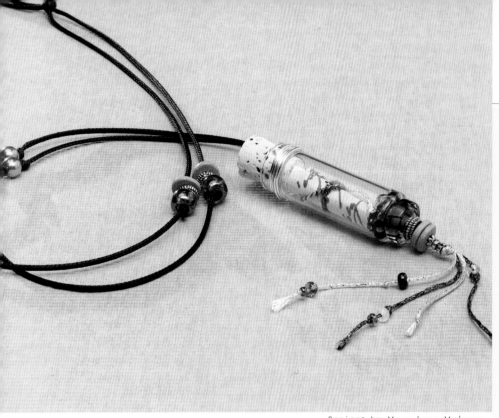

Project by *Mary Lynn Maloney*

MATERIALS

- ♥ 3/4" (19mm) glass vial with a cork
- ♥ Twenty to thirty assorted glass beads in a variety of colors
- ♥ 2"×3" (5cm × 8cm) piece of ivory card-stock
- ♥ Script rubber stamp (Stampa Rosa)
- ♥ Plum Wine archival ink (Ancient Page)
- ♥ 12" (30cm) length of metallic silver braid
- ♥ 12" (30cm) length of metallic blue/purple/pink braid
- ♥ Large-hole striped glass disc bead
- ♥ Four dark silver disc spacer beads
- ♥ Dark silver tubular spacer bead
- ♥ Two dark gold round spacer beads
- ♥ Four large-hole orange wafer beads
- ♥ Two large-hole blue glass beads
- ♥ 15" (38cm) length of 22-gauge silver wire
- ♥ 1/4" (6mm) jump ring
- ♥ 1 yard (90cm) of black nylon cord
- ♥ Wire snips
- ♥ Quick Grip permanent adhesive
- ♥ Craft glue

Maybe you can't send a friend a genie in a bottle, but you certainly can send good wishes or sweet sentiments in this charming glass vial. Beads, glitter and fibers lend lots of texture and interest to this thoughtful gift.

MESSAGE IN A BOTTLE

1 Squeeze the craft glue into the glass vial, filling the bottom of the vial with about 1/16" (2mm) of glue. Sprinkle assorted small beads into the glue to a thickness of about 1/8" (3mm). Let the mixture dry.

2 Stamp the script image onto the ivory cardstock using the plum ink or write a message of your own. Tear the cardstock to a rectangle 1 1/4" × 2" (3cm × 5cm) in size. Roll the cardstock into a scroll and tie the scroll closed with a short length of silver and multi-colored metallic braid.

3 Fold the remaining lengths of metallic braid in half. Thread the tubular bead onto the gathered strand. Then thread two orange wafer beads, one dark silver spacer bead and the large glass disc.

4 Tie a large knot against the glass disc, trimming the loose ends very closely. Push the beads together, letting the excess strands of braid hang below the tubular bead. Tie a large knot against the tubular bead, then thread assorted small glass beads onto the dangling threads. Space the beads with knots.

5 Use Quick Grip glue to attach the glass disc bead to the bottom of vial.

6 Wrap the silver wire tightly around neck of vial. Use a small dab of Quick Grip on the vial as you wrap to help secure the wire. Form a small loop in the wire for attaching the cord, and then trim the excess wire.

7 Attach jump ring to the wire loop, and then loop the black cord through the jump ring. Thread a dark silver spacer bead onto the cord and up against jump ring. Secure it with a knot. Thread the gold spacer beads, the blue glass beads and the orange wafer beads onto the black cord, securing them with knots. Determine the length of cord and tie a knot where desired.

8 Place the scroll inside the glass vial and top the vial with a cork.

MATERIALS

♥ Black craft foam

♥ Rubber stamps with bold lines (Tassel, Spiral Border and Rose Compass from All Night Media)

♥ Metallic paste in gold or silver

♥ Variety of fibers and cords

♥ Beads and charms

♥ ⅛" (3mm) hole punch

♥ Heat gun

♥ Scissors

Project by Mary Lynn Maloney

Bookmarks are great gifts for the avid reader and make wonderful additions to gift baskets. Or try giving a friend a book on her favorite subject and slip a friendship bookmark in the pages.

EMBOSSED BOOKMARKS

1 Use a heat gun to heat an area on the foam slightly larger than the stamped images. This takes about 8-10 seconds, and there should be a slight sheen to the foam when it is heated sufficiently.

2 Immediately press the rubber stamp into the heated foam. Press hard and hold it for at least 30 seconds or until the foam has cooled to room temperature.

3 If using two stamps on one bookmark, do one stamp first, then heat the area for the second stamp while avoiding the area of the first stamp as much as possible. Then impress the second stamp.

4 Trim around the embossed foam using scissors and punch a hole in the top of the bookmark.

5 Apply a light coating of metallic paste to all sides of bookmark following the manufacturer's instructions for application and drying time. Allow some of the black foam to show through in the embossed areas.

6 Cut three or four types of fibers 12" to 20" long (30cm to 51cm). Make a loop in the center of the fibers and push it through the hole in the bookmark. Pass the ends of the fibers through the loop to tie them on the bookmark. Thread beads and tie charms onto the fibers.

TIP

Choose stamps with bold lines that work well vertically. Use no more than two stamps or the process becomes complicated.

MATERIALS

- ♥ White candle
- ♥ Rub 'n Buff metallic wax in Jade
- ♥ Embossing stylus
- ♥ Glass beads
- ♥ 2' (61cm) of 18- to 22-gauge silver wire
- ♥ Rubber gloves or plastic wrap
- ♥ Soft, natural bristle brush

Transform an ordinary candle into an extraordinary gift! With metallic wax and matching glass beads, your custom candle creation will bring delight for hours of glowing beauty. This fun project is easy to create and beautiful to give.

Project by *Debba Haupert*

METALLIC CANDLE

1 Rub metallic wax over the sides of the candle. Allow the wax to dry as you complete the next step. Protect your fingers with rubber gloves or plastic wrap as you apply and emboss the metallic wax.

2 Cut a length of wire that can wrap at least three times around the candle. Add half the glass beads to the wire, and then twist the wire around one bead at the end of the

wire to secure them. Load the remaining beads onto the wire and twist the wire around the last bead at other end.

3 Use an embossing stylus to gently carve spirals into the wax. Make them deep enough that you can see the color of the candle wax. Use a soft brush to remove the excess wax.

4 Wrap the beaded wire around base of the candle.

MORE IDEAS

- Cover a candle coaster with metallic wax to match the candle.
- Draw other shapes in the wax, such as hearts, circles or words.

♥ 4' (122cm) of ⅛" (3mm) armature wire

♥ 4 to 5 yards (4m to 5m) of 26-gauge black uncoated wire

♥ Matching E beads

♥ ¾" (19mm) copper pipe cap

♥ Wire cutter

♥ Round-nose pliers

Project by Mary Lynn Maloney

Create a piece of art that doubles as a functional home accent with this bead-embellished candle snuffer. Pliable armature wire (a soft aluminum wire) creates a sturdy but easy-to-create frame. Metallic beads and wire wrapped around the base wire add color and your own personal creative touch.

HEART CANDLE SNUFFER

1 With the round-nose pliers, twist one end of the armature wire into a tight spiral. The spiral should be about ½" (13mm) in diameter.

2 Lay the flat side of the wire spiral on the closed end of the copper cap. Holding the wire firmly to the cap, begin to wrap the wire around the sides of the copper cap. Wrap the wire to the open end of the cap, and then add one last spiral. Make the last spiral slightly smaller than the cap. It should hold the cap in place.

3 The next 5" (13cm) of armature wire will form the handle of the candle snuffer. At the end of this wire, make a loop of wire about 1½" (4cm) in diameter.

4 This loop will make the heart. Use the round-nose pliers to form the center fold of the heart and make any adjustments in the wire. Then take the rest of the armature wire and loop it around the handle. When finished, make any other adjustments to the wire to make sure the snuffer will rest flat on a level surface. Bend the wire closest to the copper cap, and then cut off any wire you might have left.

5 Cut a piece of black wire about 2 yards (2m) long. Twist one end of the wire around a bead. Load 3" (8cm) of beads onto the wire.

6 Beginning at either end of the snuffer, twist the beaded wire around the armature base. Slide beads onto the wire periodically, and continue wrapping. When finished, keep the beads from sliding off the wire by twisting another bead at the end of the wire. Add another strand of wire and beads as needed.

Here's a gift that will appeal to a friend's sense of fun and sense of smell! Very simple techniques are used to create a beautifully exotic incense set packaged in rich, spicy colors. This stylish and lovely gift will have people believing you spent a fortune on the gift, but a little crafting was all you needed.

INCENSE BURNER
GIFT SET

Project by Mary Lynn Maloney

MATERIALS

- ♥ 4" × 5½" × 1" (10cm × 14cm × 3cm) white gift box with lid
- ♥ 8½" × 11" (22cm × 28cm) sheet of ivory/gold decorative paper
- ♥ 8½" × 11" (22cm × 28cm) sheet of rust mulberry paper
- ♥ Three 5" × 7" (13cm × 18cm) clear cellophane envelopes
- ♥ 4" × 6" (10cm × 15cm) ceramic tile
- ♥ Copper polymer clay
- ♥ Celtic design polymer clay mold
- ♥ One yard (90cm) each of metallic gold and metallic purple fibers
- ♥ Sandalwood and Sage archival inks (Ancient Page)
- ♥ Copper metallic pigment ink (Tsukineko)
- ♥ Forty sticks of 4" (10cm) incense
- ♥ Craft glue
- ♥ Double stick tape
- ♥ Clay blade
- ♥ Scissors
- ♥ Paintbrush
- ♥ Metallic rub-ons

1 Cut a 3" × 4" (8cm × 10cm) rectangle in the center of the white box lid. Use a brush to apply a thin layer of craft glue to the box lid, then cover it with the gold and ivory paper. Fold the paper around the edges of the rectangle cut-out and onto the back of the box top. Cover the box bottom using the craft glue and the rust mulberry paper. Let the glue dry.

2 Randomly tap the edges and corners of box lid with the sandalwood, sage and copper ink. Let the ink dry.

3 Cut a 3⅝" × 5⅛" (9cm × 13cm) rectangle from a cellophane envelope. Glue the rectangle to the inside of the box lid. Cut thin strips from the rust mulberry paper and glue it inside the box lid to cover the edges of the cellophane.

4 Put one incense stick aside, then put half of the incense sticks you have left into one of the cellophane envelopes. Cut the envelope 1" (3cm) from the edge of the incense bundle and then wrap the cellophane around the bundle. Secure the cellophane with a piece of double stick tape. Repeat this step to wrap the remaining incense sticks.

5 Wrap both bundles with a scrap of the gold and ivory paper, then a scrap of the rust mulberry paper. Secure the bundles with tape. Tie and knot each bundle with metallic fibers and trim the excess fibers.

6 Condition the polymer clay and press it into the Celtic mold. Carefully remove the clay and place it on a ceramic tile. Trim the excess clay with a blade.

7 To create an opening for the incense, use the incense stick you put aside to poke a small hole about ½" (1cm) from either end of the raw clay piece. The stick should rest at a slight angle over the strip of clay. Remove the incense stick and bake the clay according to the manufacturer's package directions. Let the clay cool, then rub the raised clay design with several colors of metallic rub-ons. Let the rubbings dry.

8 Assemble the incense bundles and burner in the covered box.

MORE IDEAS

Try using different molds for the clay. Use hearts with red clay, or a seasonal mold such as Christmas trees or wreaths. Color coordinate the clay, the decorative paper and the inks for a more personalized gift!

Project by Mary Lynn Maloney

MATERIALS

- ♥ 2½" × 3½" (6cm × 9cm) frame with an oval opening
- ♥ 4" × 5" (10cm × 13cm) sheet of light-weight ivory and gold wrapping paper
- ♥ 4" × 5" (10cm × 13cm) sheet of light-weight green metallic paper
- ♥ Costume jewelry piece
- ♥ Iridescent glue
- ♥ Gold micro-beads
- ♥ Découpage medium
- ♥ Paintbrush
- ♥ Craft glue
- ♥ Scissors

Start with an inexpensive frame and give it a touch of glitz and glamour. Use a flea market find earring as the focal point, or consider using a piece of old costume jewelry or a piece of memorabilia to make the gift really special.

BEJEWELED PHOTO FRAME

1 Remove the backing, the inner cardboard and the glass from the frame and set them aside.

2 Dilute the découpage medium with a little water and brush the medium on the lower half of frame front and sides. Tear the green metallic paper to fit the frame and adhere the paper to the front and sides of the lower half of the frame. Trim the paper where necessary and adhere it around and behind the oval opening. Brush another coat of the découpage mixture over the paper. Repeat this process with the gold wrapping paper on the upper half of the frame. Let the découpage medium dry.

3 Squeeze a thin line of iridescent glue along both long edges of frame. Sprinkle micro-beads onto the glue. Shake off the excess and let the glue dry.

4 Use craft glue to adhere a costume jewelry piece above the oval window on the frame. Let the glue dry then insert a photo and replace the glass and the frame backing.

Project by *Barbara Matthiessen*

MATERIALS

♥ Three faux ivory dominos (per holder)

♥ Green glass seed bead mix

♥ Clear and gold micro beads

♥ Rubber stamps: vine or floral background and words

♥ Solvent-based ink in olive green and black

♥ Permanent adhesive for glass and metal

♥ Dimensional adhesive

♥ Rubbing alcohol

♥ Paper towel

Everyone can use a few of these holders for displaying photographs or cards. Use them to hold business cards, small photos or a special greeting. A pair will easily hold a 5" (13cm) photograph.

DOMINO PHOTO HOLDER

1 Use rubbing alcohol and a paper towel to clean the dominos.

2 Stamp a background with olive green ink on the smooth, flat side of the dominos.

3 Use a word stamp and black ink to stamp a word across the smooth surface of the domino. Repeat steps 1 through 3 for a second domino.

4 Use dimensional adhesive to glue the bottom edges of two dominos to the flat surface of a third domino. Keep the stamped, flat surface of the upright dominos face out. Allow the glue to set.

5 Squeeze dots of dimensional adhesive onto the stamped surface of the upright dominos. Sprinkle green bead mix on the dimensional adhesive. Apply more dimensional adhesive around the edges, and sprinkle clear and then gold micro-beads. Allow the adhesive to dry and shake off the excess beads.

MORE IDEAS

■ Try holiday-themed stamps with your favorite holiday photo.

■ Use domino holders as place card holders and party favors at a get together. For example, use stamps of baby footprints for a baby shower or doves for a wedding.

■ Make holders for business cards.

■ Use sports-themed stamps to hold prized trading cards.

♥ 70" (178cm) beading wire

♥ Crimp beads

♥ Glass beads

♥ Silver prayer box charm

♥ Silver three-hole bead spacer bar

♥ Silver spacer beads

♥ Silver toggle clasp

♥ Scissors or wire cutter

Give a gift that will always be close to their heart. Colorful glass beads and antique silver accents make this necklace simple yet stylish. A personalized and inspirational message will make the gift even more meaningful.

Project by *Debba Haupert*

PRAYER BOX NECKLACE

1 Load one side of the toggle clasp onto the beading wire. Insert both ends of the wire into a crimp bead and crimp to secure the clasp in the middle of the wire.

2 Holding the ends of the wire together, string about 7" (18cm) of glass beads onto the combined wires. Add a spacer bead then divide the two wires and string 1½" (4cm) more beads onto each wire. Reunite the wires through another spacer bead and add 3" (8cm) more of glass beads onto the combined wires. Add another spacer bead and string 1" (3cm) of beads onto each wire.

3 Thread one wire through the end hole of the spacer bar. String 1" (3cm) of glass beads onto this wire then add the prayer box. String an additional 1" (3cm) of beads and feed the wire through the other end hole. String 1" (3cm) of beads onto wire.

4 Feed the other end of the wire through the center hole of the spacer bar. Add one bead, then return the wire back through the center hole. String 1" (3cm) of beads onto the end of this wire.

5 Reunite the two wires and feed them through a spacer bead. Trim the longer end of the wire so that both wires are the same length.

6 Combine the wires and string 3" (8cm) of beads on them. Add a spacer bead then string 1½" (4cm) of beads on each sepa-

rate wire. Reunite the wires through another spacer bead and string 7" (18cm) of glass beads on the combined wires.

7 For extra strength, add a crimp bead at the end of each of the wires. Slide the ends through the other end of the toggle clasp and back through the crimp beads. Crimp to secure. Trim the excess wire. Don't forget to add a note inside the prayer box!

TIP

Since the glass beads vary in size, lay the necklace flat periodically to make sure that the beads are even.

- ♥ Soft polymer clay – translucent, transparent red, transparent orange, transparent yellow, transparent blue and transparent green
- ♥ Mini heart cookie cutter
- ♥ 1½' (46cm) of 24-gauge coated wire
- ♥ Pin backing
- ♥ Craft glue
- ♥ Glue gun
- ♥ Craft knife
- ♥ Wire cutters
- ♥ Round-nose pliers
- ♥ Pasta machine or acrylic roller

Project by Debba Haupert

Creating with polymer doesn't require a lot of tools, or special skills for that matter— just a few materials and a willingness to try! This simple brooch uses a mini cookie cutter to make the inserts. Since you have to create the brooches in sets of two, you can make an extra one for yourself or another friend.

HEART BROOCH

1 Condition a block of soft translucent polymer clay. Run it through a pasta machine or work it with your hands for several minutes to soften the clay. Roll the clay into a sheet and cut it in half.

2 On a half sheet of the clay add pea-sized balls of red, yellow and orange transparent polymer clay. Fold that sheet in half with the balls of clay inside. Roll it through the pasta machine on the thickest setting, or flatten the sheet by rolling a glass or rolling pin over it. Fold the sheet in half again and repeat a few times until the colors are blended in the clay, but still show variation in the colors. Repeat this process with the other half sheet of translucent clay, but use green and blue transparent polymer balls.

3 Roll both sheets to approximately ⅛" to 1/16" (3mm to 2mm) thick. This is the thickest setting on the pasta machine. Cut two 1½" × 2" (4cm × 5cm) squares from each sheet.

4 Cut a heart from the center of each square using a mini cookie cutter. Gently remove the center hearts and replace each heart with the heart from the other sheet.

5 Gently roll and press the polymer clay sheets to attach the heart and background pieces. Use a wire to make three holes at the bottom of the squares. Use the remaining clay to shape mini hearts ¼" and ⅛" (6mm and 3mm) thick. Press a hole in the hearts with wire. Bake the clay according to the manufacturer's guidelines. Let the clay cool.

6 For each brooch, cut three 3" (8cm) pieces of wire. Insert the wire in the holes beneath the heart and twist one end around other half of the wire. With the remaining end, insert in mini hearts and twist the end to secure. Trim the excess wire.

7 Glue a pin back to the polymer clay with a glue gun. Allow the glue to dry before you use the pin.

TIP

Polymer clay is very safe, but you shouldn't reuse your cookie cutter with food after a polymer clay project. Keep tools on hand that are just for polymer clay.

Project by *Mary Lynn Maloney*

MATERIALS

- ♥ 3" × 5" (8cm × 13cm) piece of medium green cardstock
- ♥ 3" × 5" (8cm × 13cm) piece of rust cardstock
- ♥ 12" (30cm) length of ³⁄₈" (9mm) sage green satin ribbon
- ♥ Two LOVE postage stamps
- ♥ Two large-hole amber beads
- ♥ Gold gel pen
- ♥ Gold leafing pen
- ♥ Clear dimensional adhesive
- ♥ Glue stick
- ♥ Metal edge ruler
- ♥ Pin
- ♥ Craft knife
- ♥ Scissors

A gift of love suits any occasion. This practical bookmark would make a beautiful Valentine's Day, birthday or anniversary gift, as well as a unique wedding favor.

L O V E   B O O K M A R K

1 Adhere a LOVE stamp onto the green cardstock. Using a ruler and a craft knife, trim the cardstock, leaving approximately a ¹⁄₈" (3mm) border around the stamp.

2 Glue the assembled piece onto the rust cardstock and trim, leaving a slightly larger border around green cardstock. Cut two more rectangles of rust cardstock the same size. Adhere a second LOVE stamp to a piece of rust cardstock the same size as the green cardstock.

3 Cover the LOVE stamps with a thin layer of clear dimensional adhesive. Pop any air bubbles in the adhesive with a pin. Let the adhesive dry thoroughly.

4 Using a gold gel pen, write a special message on the plain rust cardstock rectangles. Edge the border of the rust rectangles with a gold leafing pen. Let the ink dry.

5 Thread a large-hole bead onto one end of the ribbon and knot the ribbon to secure the bead. Trim the ribbon end into points.

Repeat with the remaining bead on the other end of the ribbon.

6 Apply a generous layer of glue from the glue stick to the back of an assembled LOVE stamp piece and to a cardstock piece with your written message. Just above a bead, sandwich the ribbon between these two pieces and press firmly to adhere. Repeat this step with the remaining cardstock pieces at the opposite end of ribbon.

Project by *Mary Lynn Maloney*

MATERIALS

- $7/8$" × $1 7/8$" (22mm × 5cm) ivory colored domino
- $1/2$" × $1 1/4$" (13mm × 3cm) brass dog tag
- Two iridescent green wafer beads
- Amethyst glass bead, matte green bead and brass tubular spacer bead
- One yard (90cm) of black nylon cord
- Scroll rubber stamp (Penny Black)
- Leaf Green, Jade and Deep Harbor archival inks (Ancient Page)
- Pink, orange and blue chalk pastels
- Copper leafing pen
- Matte spray sealer
- Permanent glue
- Fine grit sandpaper
- $1 1/2$" (4cm) silver eye pin
- $1/4$" (6mm) brass jump ring
- Wire snips
- Hand or Dremel drill with $1/32$" (.8mm) bit
- Safety goggles
- Scissors

Treat the blank side of a domino like a mini canvas and create this small work of art. Some unexpected materials come together to form a unique piece of jewelry sure to be appreciated by a friend with an artistic eye.

DOG TAG DOMINO PENDANT

1 Lightly sand the blank side of the domino. Wash the domino and wipe it dry.

2 Dab Leaf Green ink randomly onto the sanded surface of the domino. Don't forget to ink the edges of the domino as well. Repeat with the Jade ink. Dab some of the ink off the domino with a rag, then let the domino dry.

3 Apply Deep Harbor ink to the rubber stamp. Press the sanded side of the domino onto the stamp. Remove the domino and let it dry. Spray the domino with a light coat of matte sealer.

4 Use your fingers to rub touches of the chalk pastel colors onto the domino. Gently layer the colors for more depth and interest. Spray the domino with matte sealer and let the sealer dry.

5 Run a copper leafing pen along the edges and front corners of the domino. Let the ink dry, then spray it again with matte sealer.

6 Attach the dog tag to the right side of the domino using the permanent glue. Adhere the two green wafer beads over the holes in the dog tag. Let the glue dry.

7 Drill a hole slightly to the left of center on the top edge of the domino. Thread the matte green and amethyst beads onto the eye pin. Trim the eye pin and dip it into the glue. Insert the eye pin into the domino and let it dry.

8 Attach a brass jump ring to the eye pin and loop the nylon cord through it. Thread the brass tubular bead onto the cord and secure it above jump ring with a knot. Adjust the cord to the desired length and tie off the neck end with a knot. Trim any excess cord.

TIP

Protect your eyes and wear safety goggles when you are drilling into the domino.

- ♥ Canvas memory book cover
- ♥ $4\frac{1}{2}$" × 6" (11cm × 15cm) piece of mat board
- ♥ ¼ yard (22cm) light and dark blue striped fabric
- ♥ ¼ yard (22cm) blue paisley print fabric
- ♥ 18" (46cm) length of fuzzy blue trim
- ♥ 12" (30cm) length of off-white textured fiber
- ♥ 12" (30cm) length of ¼" (6mm) blue satin ribbon
- ♥ 12" (30cm) length of colorful yarn
- ♥ Two buttons
- ♥ Baby theme applique
- ♥ Fabric glue
- ♥ Scissors

Project by Mary Lynn Maloney

The canvas album cover used for this gift is ready-made—just waiting for your decorative touch! The embellishment shown here has baby in mind, but you can tailor it to your particular special event.

BABY MEMORY BOOK COVER

1 Cut the striped fabric to the size of the mat board with an additional 2" (5cm) around the edges.

2 Lay the fabric right side down. Apply fabric glue to one side of the mat board, and place the glued side of the mat board against the fabric. Make sure the fabric is smooth. Cover the board with the fabric. Fold and miter the corners to reduce the bulk.

3 Cut a strip of paisley fabric to 3" × 10" (8cm × 25cm) and glue it over the striped fabric along the right-hand side of the mat board. Wrap the fabric over the edge of the board, and fold and miter the corners.

4 Glue the fuzzy blue trim along the line where the fabrics meet, covering any raw edges. Glue the satin ribbon at the top of the trim, and then glue off-white fiber on top of satin ribbon. Bring all trims to back of board as you go and secure them to the mat board.

5 Glue a baby theme applique onto the assembled fabric-covered board. Glue the entire piece onto the album cover. Slip the padded cover onto the photo album or scrapbook of choice.

6 Weave the colorful yarn through the 12" (30cm) of fuzzy blue trim. Use the fabric glue to attach the fuzzy blue trim to the edge of the memory book cover. Glue buttons on either end of the fuzzy blue trim.

MATERIALS

- 5" × 6½" (13cm × 17cm) pre-purchased photo album with stiff paperboard cover

- 13¼" × 6¾" (34cm × 17cm) piece of light brown oil-tanned craft leather

- 1¾" × 1¾" (4cm × 4cm) piece of light brown oil-tanned craft leather

- Two ⅜" × 9" (9mm × 23cm) light brown suede strips

- ¾" × 10" (19mm × 25cm) light brown suede strip

- 4½" × 6¼" (11cm × 16cm) piece of handmade paper

- Four to six vintage travel-themed stickers (Stampa Rosa)

- Craft glue

- Leather cement or adhesive

- Glue paintbrush

- Large sheet of scrap paper

- Heavy-duty scissors

Project by *Mary Lynn Maloney*

A humble, inexpensive photo album is transformed into a vintage suitcase that recalls the memory of vacations past. This is a great gift for a friend who's been bitten by the travel bug. The soft leather album is an ideal way to display photos from a favorite journey.

VINTAGE SUITCASE
PHOTO ALBUM

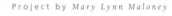

1 Lay the 13¼" × 6¾" (34cm × 17cm) light brown oil-tanned leather face down on large scrap of paper. Brush the back of the leather with leather cement. Lay the open photo album, cover side down, on top of the leather and carefully wrap the leather over the entire album, covering the front, spine and back of the album. Make sure there are no lumps or folds in the leather. Bend the album closed to get a smooth covering of leather. Gently open and close the album several times as it dries.

2 Place the album with the spine at the bottom and glue the two ⅜" × 9" (9mm × 23cm) strips of light brown suede vertically down the front of the album, about 1" (3cm) from outer edges. Wrap the suede around the album to the back, creating the luggage straps.

3 Create the luggage handle by gluing the two ends of the ¾" × 10" (19mm × 25cm) strip of light brown suede to the inside front cover, letting the fold of leather hang out of the album.

4 Use craft glue to cover the front inside cover, where the handles have been attached, with a piece of handmade paper.

5 Cut the 1¾" (4cm) square piece of leather in half, so you have two triangles of leather. Use the leather cement to glue these so the fuzzy leather side is on the outside corners of the cover.

6 Cut out the vintage travel stickers and adhere them randomly to the front of the "suitcase."

MATERIALS

♥ Red soft polymer clay

♥ Polymer varnish

♥ 18-gauge coated wire

♥ 1¼" (3cm) cork

♥ Drill with ⅜" (9mm) drill bit

♥ Wire cutter

♥ Round-nose pliers

♥ Awl

Project by *Mary Lynn Maloney*

Personalize your gift of gourmet vinegar, wine or bath oil with a heartfelt touch. No previous polymer or wire experience necessary – just cook up a little clay, arrange it on some free-form wire and secure your creation in a simple cork. Perfect as a hostess gift or to accompany a pampering present. This decorative cork is fun to create, give and receive.

HEART CORK

1 Condition the clay by softening it in your hands or with a pasta machine, then shape it into two hearts, 1" × 1" × ¼" (3cm × 3cm × 6mm).

2 Use an awl or wire to create a vertical hole lengthwise through the heart, and then bake the clay according to the manufacturer's guidelines. Allow the clay to cool before continuing.

3 Paint the heart with a polymer varnish. Let the clay dry and then repeat so there are two coats of varnish on the hearts.

4 Drill a ½" (13mm) deep hole in the center of the cork.

5 Cut a 7" (18cm) piece of wire. Twist several curls on one end of the wire. Thread a heart on the wire, letting it rest on the curl. Continue curling the wire beneath the heart, but leave about ½" (13mm) uncurled at the end.

6 Insert the uncurled end of the wire into the hole in the cork. Repeat steps 5 and 6 with the other heart using a 6" (15cm) piece of wire. Afterwards, cut three more pieces of wire between 4" and 6" (10cm and 15cm) in length. Twist and curl each of these and insert them into the cork.

MORE IDEAS

■ Make other shapes and colors, such as gold stars or purple grapes.

■ Roll the polymer clay out flat and use cookie cutters to make shapes.

■ Embellish the wire with colorful beads and/or multi-colored wire.

■ Make a mini version for perfume, bath oil or bath salts.

For One Charm

♥ Shrink plastic

♥ ⅛" (3mm) hole punch

♥ Jump rings

♥ 6" (15cm) of 24-gauge wire

♥ Seed beads, ⅛" (3mm) diameter (24 per charm)

♥ Fine tip permanent markers

♥ Wire cutters

♥ Round-nose pliers

Project by *Drenda Barker*

The perfect accessory to have at your next party! Personalized wine glass charms are fun and make a great favor for the guest to take home after the party. Add a splash to the project with colorful seed beads.

BEADED WINE CHARMS

TO MAKE THE PERSONALIZED NAME TAG

1 Use the template on page 91 and trace the oval on a piece of shrink plastic. Trace one oval for each wine charm you will make.

2 Using permanent markers, write a guest's name on the shrink plastic.

3 Use the ⅛" (3mm) hole punch to make a hole at one end of the oval. Be careful not to punch too close to the edge.

4 Follow manufacturer's directions for shrinking the plastic. The 2¼" (6cm) oval should shrink to about ⅞" (22mm).

5 Attach a jump ring through the hole. Do this for each of the charms.

TO MAKE THE WINE CHARM

1 Using round-nose pliers, make a loop at one end of the wire, wrapping the excess wire as close as you can around the loop.

2 String the beads onto the wire.

3 To close the loop and secure the beads, measure ¼"(6mm) of wire after last the bead. Bend the wire back to form a hook and wrap the end around the wire, as close as you can to the last bead. Use wire cutters to snip off any excess wire.

4 Attach the personalized name tag by attaching the jump ring to the wire loop. To close the wire ring, insert the hook into the loop and form a circle.

G I F T S   F O R
T H E   H O M E

A HOME IS MORE THAN SIMPLY AN ADDRESS—IT'S A SANCTUARY. It's a tool of self-expression where whims and dreams can be brought to life. It's a refuge from the manic and a creative retreat from the world. It can be a place to entertain, enjoy, relax and escape.

The home is a perfect place to let your creative gifts find root. Your friends and family would love having something you made in their home.

Turn the pages to find an elegant lavender banner created with a simple acrylic glaze and muslin, wound with a gorgeous ribbon and embellished with tranquil bundles of dried lavender. Place the banner by a door or window and let a gentle breeze do the work. Or how about a bulletin board to store notes, or a key box for protecting your keepsakes? You can find all that and more in these pages. With a bit of wire and some simple tools, you can create a wind chime. With some polymer clay and memorabilia from the beach, you can create a striking glass votive that is sure to become a conversation piece.

Take a moment to let your mind wander through this section and see what gifts are waiting to be made.

♥ ½ yard (50cm) of 45" (114cm) wide muslin fabric

♥ Five yards (5m) of 1" (3cm) wide sheer white ribbon

♥ 12" (30cm) long ⅜" (9mm) dowel

♥ Soft green and lavender acrylic paint

♥ Assorted green glass beads

♥ Dried bundles of lavender

♥ ½ yard (50cm) of iron-on adhesive

♥ Fabric glue

♥ Scissors

♥ Iron

♥ Plastic bucket

♥ Ruler or measuring tape

No scent is more relaxing than lavender— making this banner ideal for anyone seeking tranquility. Place this banner by a door or window with subtle airflow, and the soft scent will fill the room.

Project by Barbara Matthiessen

LAVENDER BANNER

1 Tear the fabric by clipping the fabric edges with scissors and then pulling the sides apart. Tear one 11" × 39" (28cm × 99cm) and three 5½" × 8" (14cm × 20cm) pieces of muslin.

2 In a bucket or bowl mix 1 oz. (28grams) of green paint with 2 cups (.47 liters) of water. Place the 11" (28cm) wide fabric into the paint glaze and swirl it around. Squeeze out the excess paint and hang the muslin to dry. Repeat this step using the lavender paint with the three 5½" (14cm) wide fabrics.

3 Iron the muslin pieces to remove wrinkles.

4 Attach the lavender muslin pieces to one side of the iron-on adhesive following the manufacturer's instructions. Peel off the backing paper, then place the lavender pieces evenly spaced down the center of the green fabric. The bottom lavender piece is 2¾" (7cm) up from the bottom, and the next two are spaced 2" (5cm) apart, one above the other. Iron them in place.

5 Lay the dowel against the back of the muslin near the top, and then fold 1½" (4cm) of muslin over the dowel. Glue this loop of muslin in place, securing the dowel inside the rolled fabric.

6 Cut three 24" (61cm) lengths of ribbon. Glue the center of each ribbon to the center of each piece of lavender fabric. Loop and knot 50" (127cm) of ribbon around the ends of the dowel to form a hanger with streamers from either side. Cut the streamers into three strands, and add beads to the dowel ends and the streamers.

7 Tie bundles of lavender to the banner with the three lengths of ribbon. Wrap the ribbon tightly around each bundle, and then tie a bow with the ends of the ribbon. Replace the lavender when necessary to keep the banner fresh.

MORE IDEAS

■ Make a rustic banner from burlap by tying on rosemary, sage or other herbs for a house-warming gift.

■ Try using winter holiday fabrics and tying on sprigs of evergreen.

Project by Debba Haupert

MATERIALS

- ♥ Soft translucent polymer clay
- ♥ Colored or natural sand
- ♥ Mini shells and sea glass
- ♥ Glass container or votive
- ♥ Craft knife
- ♥ Pasta machine or clay roller

This polymer candleholder can make you a mosaic artist within an hour. The secret to this speedy but stunning creation is polymer "grout." Gather some sea glass and shells and mosaic the easy way!

MOSAIC CANDLEHOLDER

1 Condition the clay with pasta machine or by hand rolling it. Make a sheet of polymer roughly ¼" (6mm) thick, slightly longer than the distance around the glass container and 3" (8cm) wide.

2 Lay the polymer clay onto the top edge of the glass votive. Stretch and press the clay till it lies flat. Cut the clay where it overlaps and press the edges together to seal the seam. Use a craft knife to trim the polymer clay and to scallop around the top of the container.

3 Firmly press pieces of sea glass and shells into the polymer clay. Smooth the polymer clay around the edges of the glass and shells to secure them.

4 Pour sand in a pan or plastic bag. Roll the votive in the sand, pressing the sand into the polymer clay.

5 Bake the clay following the manufacturer's guidelines. Allow the clay to cool, and then add colored sand inside to hold your candle.

MORE IDEAS

- Add glass beads or flat marbles to the polymer clay for more color options.
- Include shells with the sand inside the container, or use multiple colors of sand and layer them in the glass.

MATERIALS

Friendship Pot

♥ 3¼" (8cm) square flowerpot

♥ Light blue and green pigment inkpads (Brilliance Pearlized Sky Blue from Tsukineko and New Green from Colorbox)

♥ Rubber stamps (Acorn Border from All Night Media and Devotion Slab from Postmodern Design)

♥ Clear acrylic sealer

Impressions Pot

♥ 3¼" (8cm) square flowerpot

♥ Red, clay and light green inkpads (Tuscany Petal Point from Colorbox)

♥ Black inkpad

♥ Rubber stamps (Leaf from Stamp in Hand and Square Stripes from All Night Media)

♥ Clear acrylic sealer

Project by Barbara Matthiessen

Decorated square pots can be used in nearly every room of the house for storing small items, to hold a houseplant or as a festive accent. Fill the pots with bags of candy, hair ornaments, colored pencils or hobby items such as seed packets or golf balls with tees for a pleasing gift.

SQUARE FLOWERPOTS

FOR THE FRIENDSHIP POT

1 Rub inks directly from the inkpad onto the pot. Rub the blue ink on the top of the pot, and the green on the bottom. Blend the inks together with your finger. Allow the inks to dry.

2 Stamp a blue border around the base of pot, and then stamp words above the border.

3 To use the pots for live plants, spray them when completed with a clear acrylic sealer.

FOR THE IMPRESSIONS POT

1 Rub inks directly from the inkpad onto the pot. Rub the red ink on the top of the pot, the orange in the middle and the green on the bottom. Blend the inks together with your finger. Allow the inks to dry.

2 Use black ink to stamp a square design in center of each side. Stamp leaves across the top and bottom.

3 To use the pots for live plants, spray them when completed with a clear acrylic sealer.

Project by Debba Haupert

Frame a favorite photo with colorful silk flowers and a personalized message. Customize it with special colors and the names of your friends in alphabet beads. The perfect gift for the best friend who makes your life more beautiful just by being in it!

F L O W E R F R A M E

1 String 2" (5cm) of glass beads onto a 10" (25cm) length of yarn. Then continue to load alphabet beads to spell out "Best Friends." Use a glass bead to separate the words. String an additional 2" (5cm) of glass beads after the words.

2 Center the beaded yarn beneath the picture opening and hot glue the ends of the yarn to the frame.

3 Pull flower buds off silk flower stems, and then remove the plastic base behind the flowers. Hot glue the buds to the frame. Make sure to cover the glued ends of the yarn with flowers.

4 Take a few buds apart and use the individual petals, folded in half and then in half again, to make into a smaller flower. Use these to fill in space around the buds.

5 If your silk buds are thick, the glue may not reach the top layers. Remove any flowers that are loose and reattach them with the hot glue gun. Allow the glue to cool.

TIP

If you are having trouble adding beads to the yarn, use a piece of wire like a needle. Fold the wire in half at one end of your yarn, with the yarn against the wire, and then load the beads on the wire first.

Boxes are magical vessels made to hold treasures, everyday items or other gifts while they add style to any room. This simple, elegant box done in natural tones and a repeated key motif is suitable for any gift-giving occasion.

ALL KEYED UP BOX

Project by Barbara Matthiessen

MATERIALS

- 6" (15cm) square wood box with lid and ball knob
- 1½" (4cm) brass key charm
- Three small manila shipping tags
- Beige, brown, tan and black fibers
- Watermark, brown and black inkpads (Versamark, Brilliance Tiramisu and Versafine Onyx Black from Tsukineko)
- Rubber stamps (Crackle Background from Son Light Impressions, Large Key from Rubber Stampede, Small Keys from Impression Obsession and Script from Stampers Anonymous)
- 2" (5cm) of 18-gauge copper wire
- Clear spray and sealer
- Drill with small bit
- Soft bristle paintbrush
- Paper towel
- Scissors

1 Drill a small hole in the center of the front panel of the box lid. You will attach a charm to it later. Wipe away the dust with a damp paper towel.

2 Stamp a crackle background on the surface of the box using Watermark ink. Make sure you stamp the ball knob as well. Allow the ink to dry.

3 Dab a soft bristle brush into the brown ink, and then brush over the Watermark stamped background to bring out the cracks. Allow this inking to be uneven.

4 Rub brown ink directly onto the box edges, including the corners. Apply a second, heavier coat of ink to the ball knob.

5 Use brown ink and the script stamp to stamp the tags.

6 Stamp brown, large keys all over the box and tags. Position keys in different directions, and stamp some off the top, bottom and side edges.

7 Rub all the tag edges with the brown inkpad. You can also write messages on the tags.

8 As a top layer, stamp smaller keys over the box using black ink. Allow the inks to dry.

9 Spray two coats of sealer over the box following the manufacturer's instructions for application and drying time.

10 Thread a key onto wire and insert the wire through the drilled hole. Twist the wire into a spiral knot inside the lid.

11 Cut a variety of fibers from 14" to 24" (36cm to 61cm) long. Gather the fiber centers together and fold them in half. Insert the fold through the holes in the tags. Run the fiber ends through the loop formed by fold, and then pull down evenly. Tie the fibers around the ball knob.

MORE IDEAS

- Design a box around clocks using clock rubber stamps and clock parts.
- Use postage stamps, real and rubber stamped, to make a great stationery box.

MATERIALS

- ♥ 13½" × 10½" (34cm × 27cm) document frame

- ♥ 14" × 11" (36cm × 28cm) piece of posterboard

- ♥ 15½" × 12½" (39cm × 32cm) piece of decorative paper or fabric

- ♥ Four 16" (41cm) lengths of ¼" wide (6mm) ribbon

- ♥ Four 9" (23cm) lengths of ¼" wide (6mm) ribbon

- ♥ Three 3¾" (10cm) brass cup hooks

- ♥ Eight mini brass brads

- ♥ Glue stick

- ♥ Craft glue

- ♥ Measuring tape or ruler

- ♥ Awl

- ♥ Pencil

Project by *Drenda Barker*

Create this message center with fabric or paper that coordinates with a room's decor. The cup hooks on the bottom make it easy to pick up keys and review notes while you're running out the door.

FRENCH BULLETIN BOARD

1 Remove the back of the document frame and the glass. You will not need the glass for this project. Then use the glue stick to cover the posterboard with decorative paper or fabric.

2 Measure and mark the 14" (36cm) sides of covered posterboard every 4⅔" (12cm), creating three equal sections. Measure and mark the 11" (28cm) every 5½" (14cm), creating two equal sections.

3 Draw lines lightly on posterboard marking the sections you just made. Start at a 4⅔" (12cm) point and make a line to the 5½" (14cm) mark on the nearest side. At the next 4⅔" (12cm) make a line to the opposite corner. Then at the corner, make a line to the 4⅔" (12cm) point on the opposite side. Finally, make a line from the middle 5½" (14cm) to the last 4⅔" (12cm) point. Continue this pattern, only in the opposite direction, to divide the posterboard into diamonds.

4 Lay ribbon on the lines you just made, securing the ends with craft glue. Secure one end first, and then the other. Lay ribbon in one direction first, and then in the other.

5 At each point where the ribbon intersects use the awl to make a hole in the ribbon and posterboard. Then, insert a brad through the hole and secure it on the back of the posterboard.

6 Fold the ribbon hanging over the edge of the board to the back and secure it with craft glue. The back side of the board will be covered with the back of the document frame, so you don't have to spend a lot of time making it pretty.

7 Replace the back of document frame with the poster board. Attach cup hooks to the bottom of the frame. Use an awl to start a hole where a cup hook will be, and then screw the cup hook in the hole.

♥ Wood tray

♥ Photocopies of letters, notes, postcards and postage stamps

♥ Ivory acrylic paint

♥ Découpage medium

♥ Craft glue

♥ Medium to fine grit sand-paper

♥ 1" (3cm) wide paintbrush

♥ Scissors

♥ Felt to cover bottom of tray

♥ Paper towel

Project by Barbara Matthiessen

Isn't it amazing how a postcard can remind you of a great vacation or trip? Old letters and cards bring back pleasant memories on this useful and nostalgic project. Add copies of old memorabilia such as birth certificates to make this gift even more special or create a theme tray around other events.

VINTAGE CORRESPONDENCE **TRAY**

1 Sand any rough edges on the tray. If it has already been painted, then sand to remove the paint gloss. Wipe off the tray when finished with a damp paper towel.

2 Paint the entire tray ivory. Allow the paint to dry.

3 Plan your design by placing correspondence, such as letters, on your tray's background. Tear some edges of the correspondence, and trim others with scissors. Do not adhere any pieces until you know how you will arrange the papers.

4 Apply papers to the tray one at a time using découpage medium and following your layout. Brush a coat of découpage medium onto the tray and the back of the papers. Place the papers onto the tray. Smooth out the paper using a brush wet with découpage medium. When all papers have been applied, brush on two more coats of medium allowing drying time in between coats.

5 Découpage the sides of the tray using any leftover pieces, and glue felt to the bottom of the tray using craft glue.

TIP

Preserve important documents from your past by making photo or color copies before you begin your projects.

Project by Barbara Matthiessen

Want a clock that will fit anywhere? You can quickly and inexpensively make distinctive clocks no one else on the block will have. Choose the right theme and the clock can be a fantastic conversation piece and the focal point of a room.

COLLAGE CLOCK

1 Apply a thin layer of dimensional adhesive to the CD, then add strips of sheet music to cover the CD. This will be the background.

2 Apply two more coats of dimensional adhesive over the sheet music, then allow the CD to dry.

3 Apply more dimensional adhesive, then add postage stamps and numbers around the clock face.

4 Apply two more coats of dimensional adhesive over the CD and allow it to dry.

5 Assemble the clock following the manufacturer's instructions. The clockworks will fit through the hole in the center of the CD. Make sure to add a metal washer on top of the CD before screwing on the hex nut.

MORE IDEAS

Choose a theme for your clock and then add a background and embellishments to match the theme. For example, try a nature theme or a heritage clock with pictures of family. Just make sure the background and embellishments do not interfere with the clockworks.

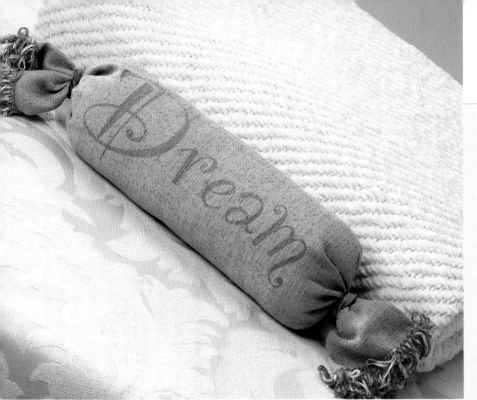

Project by *Mary Lynn Maloney*

MATERIALS

- 14" x 22" (36cm x 56cm) piece of loosely woven cotton or cotton blend fabric in sage green
- Premium glossy photo paper and inkjet printer
- Two yards of gold/green fuzzy fringe trim
- Two 12" (30cm) lengths of 1" (3cm) wide olive green silk ribbon
- Polyester stuffing
- Two tablespoons of lavender flower buds
- Blue Gold pearlescent fabric paint
- Matte spray sealer
- Fabric glue
- Spray bottle of water
- Bone folder
- Iron
- Rag
- Paintbrush
- Scissors
- Measuring tape or ruler

The size of this no-sew pillow makes it ideal for a little cat nap. Lavender flowers sprinkled inside the pillow stuffing encourages relaxation and calm.

DREAM PILLOW

TO MAKE THE TRANSFER

To create the transfer for this project, type the word "Dream" in a word processing program. Choose the "flip horizontal" in the print dialog box. Print onto an inkjet premium glossy photo paper. The word should be reversed. Do not use any photo paper that is quick drying. Directions may vary between computers and printers.

TO MAKE THE PILLOW

1 Lay the sage green fabric on a flat work surface with the 22" (56cm) edges at top and bottom. Mist with water from spray bottle. Lay the printed photo paper face down in the middle of the fabric and smooth so there are no wrinkles. Spray the back of the photo paper with a mist of water. Burnish the back of the paper with a bone folder. You can lift up the corner of the paper to peek at progress of transfer. If the transfer looks too light after about 45 seconds, spray a tiny bit more water onto the fabric and continue burnishing.

2 Remove the photo paper. Dab up any slightly gooey emulsion left behind by the paper with a damp rag. Do not dab the transfer itself! Let the fabric dry thoroughly. Use the paintbrush and pearlescent paint to add dots and highlight lines to the transferred word. Let the paint dry. Spray with a light coat of matte spray sealer.

3 Cut two 15" (38cm) lengths of fuzzy fringe trim and glue it along the edges of the 14" (36cm) sides of sage green fabric. Trim any excess fringe.

4 Fold the 22" (56cm) edges ⅜" (9mm) in toward the back of fabric. Press along the fold with an iron, then glue the pressed edge down.

5 Turn fabric on its back. Lay a handful of the polyester stuffing in the center of the fabric and shape it to an approximately 14" x 5" (36cm x 13cm) roll. Sprinkle the lavender into the stuffingl roll. Roll the fabric around the stuffing so that the word "Dream" will become the front of the pillow. Glue the edge down; the seam side will be the back of the pillow.

6 Gather up the edges of the rolled pillow 3½" (9cm) from the fuzzy fringed edge. Tightly wrap and tie the gathered sections with the olive ribbon, using small dabs of glue to secure the knot and the ribbon to the pillow.

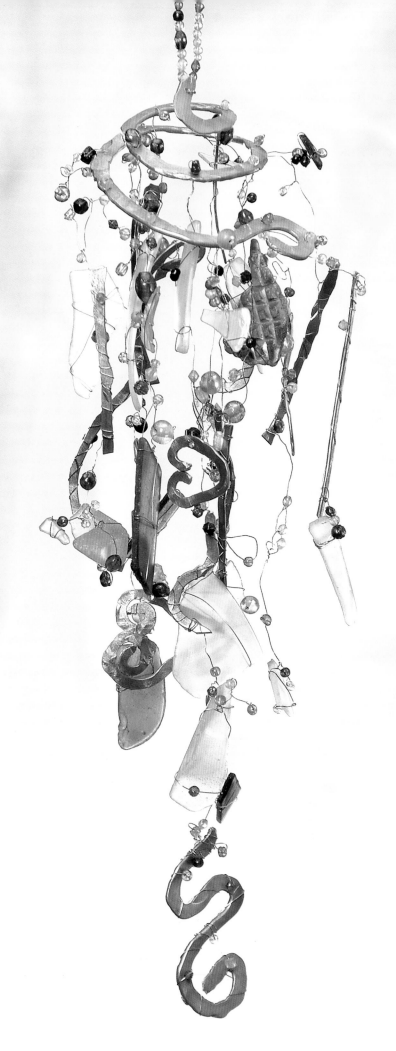

Don't let the use of a few tools stand between you and this beautiful gift. A hammer, drill and wire cutter are easy to use, and in no time at all you can create a wonderful and unique gift. On a sunny day or windy afternoon, this gift will remind someone special of your beautiful friendship.

WIND CHIME

MATERIALS

- ♥ 10' (3m) of 3/16" (5mm) armature wire
- ♥ 26-gauge colored wire
- ♥ Sea glass
- ♥ Matching glass beads
- ♥ 3/4" (19mm) silver jingle bells
- ♥ Hammer
- ♥ Anvil or surface on which to hammer
- ♥ Drill with 1/16" (2mm) drill bit
- ♥ Metal file
- ♥ Marker
- ♥ Heavy-duty wire cutter
- ♥ Round-nose pliers
- ♥ Ear protection

1 Hold one end of a 4' (122cm) length of armature wire with the pliers and twist it into a circle about the size of a quarter. Continue manually making a flat spiral with the armature, increasing each ring so that the final spiral is 7" (18cm) in diameter. Twist the outside end of the wire into another quarter-sized curl.

2 With the remaining armature wire, cut random links ranging from 3" to 6" (8cm to 15cm) long. Create twelve to sixteen links this way. Bend the longer lengths into squiggles or hearts using the pliers.

3 Make sure you wear ear protection for this step. Place the spiral on an anvil or a vise. Hammer the spiral to flatten the armature wire. Hold the wire with pliers while you

hammer for safety. Strike the wire at different angles for a more textured look. Turn the spiral over periodically to maintain the general flatness of the spiral. Different angles give it personality, so don't worry about making it perfectly flat.

4 Repeat the last step with each of the links. Flatten the wire to roughly 1/4" to 3/8" (6mm to 9mm) wide.

5 Use a marker to indicate on the spiral where the strands should hang. Starting at the outermost end, place a hole 2" (5cm) in from the outside curled end of the wire. Place random holes on the spiral approximately every 3" to 4" (8cm to 10cm) until you have eight to ten holes. Make one hole in the center of the spiral. This will be the hook for hanging your wind chime.

6 Place the spiral over an old board or on a surface you won't damage and drill holes in the spiral as marked in the last step. Then drill one or two holes in each of the hammered wire lengths and shapes. Use the metal file to smooth any rough edges.

7 Create the hanging strands with 3' to 4' (92cm to 122cm) lengths of the thin, colored wire. Insert one end of this wire through the hole in the armature links and twist to secure. Begin randomly placing beads, bells, sea glass and hammered wire pieces wrapped on the thin wire.

Twist the beads to space them apart on the wire. Wrap the wire around the sea glass and twist to tighten and secure. Continue adding decorative embellishments, ending each strand with a hammered armature wire piece.

8 Feed the end of the strands up through the holes in the bottom of the spiral. Add a bead, and then stick the wire back through the hole and twist the top of the strand to secure it. Gently adjust the base spiral if it hangs at an angle. Note: Armature wire is stronger once hammered but also is more likely to break if bent very much, so be careful when balancing.

9 Continue attaching the strands to the spiral. With a 6" (15cm) piece of the thin wire, load about 3" (8cm) of beads and bend to form a loop. Twist and insert this in center of the spiral to create a hanger.

TIP

To avoid tangles when wrapping, place tissue paper between strands. Gently lay the wind chime in a gift bag with the beaded loop positioned to lift out.

Project by Debba Haupert

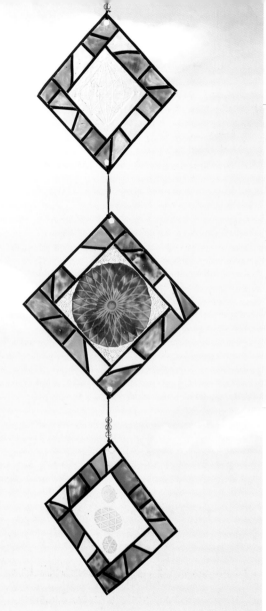

MATERIALS

- ♥ Two 5" (13cm) and one 6" (15cm) clear acrylic squares (a good substitute is heat-resistant acetate)
- ♥ Bevel Mold (Gallery Glass)
- ♥ Crystal Beads (Gallery Glass)
- ♥ Silver Redi-Lead Strips (Gallery Glass)
- ♥ Silver Liquid Lead (Gallery Glass)
- ♥ Window Color Crystal Clear, Emerald Green, Sapphire, Bright Blue and Blue Diamond (Gallery Glass)
- ♥ 2' (61cm) green 3mm ribbon
- ♥ Seven 8mm crystal faceted beads
- ♥ Hole punch
- ♥ Toothpick
- ♥ Scissors

Add sparkle and color to any window, door or wall with this hanger using glass color, faux leading and beads. Get a jump start on your crafting by making up a number of bevels the night before.

SUN CATCHER

1 To make the center of the sun catcher, fill the bevel molds with Window Color. Make one large and three small clear bevels, and one large blue bevel. Use a toothpick to break any bubbles and to move glass color into the corners and grooves. Set it aside to dry. It should take 2 – 8 hours, depending on the temperature and humidity.

2 Punch two holes, in diagonally opposite corners, in one 5" (13cm) and the 6" (15cm) clear acrylic squares. Punch one corner hole in the remaining 5" (13cm) square. These squares will be the foundation of your sun catcher.

3 Create a frame around the acrylic squares by pressing the lead strips around the edge of the squares. Cut the leading strips with scissors and press the strips tightly together. Do not stretch them. Measure 1" (3cm) in from edge on all the acrylic squares and create a second, smaller frame by applying the lead strips on the acrylic square.

4 In the space between the outer and inner frame use the lead strips to create panes. Each of the lead strips creating the panes should touch both the inner and outer frame. Apply a dot of Liquid Lead to each lead strip intersection. Allow the Liquid Lead to dry.

5 Peel the dried center decorations out of the bevel molds, and then press them onto the center of the acrylic squares. Place the blue bevel on the 6" (15cm) square. Fill the remaining area between the decoration and the inner frame with clear glass color. Sprinkle clear beads into the wet glass color around the blue decoration.

6 Fill in the panes using various colors of Window Color. Allow the frame to dry completely.

7 Tie the ribbon onto one 5" (13cm) square, thread on a crystal bead and then tie the ribbon into a hanging loop. Cut additional pieces of ribbon to join the remaining squares. Tie ribbons through punched holes on 6" (15cm) square, thread on three beads, and then tie it onto the 5" (13cm) squares. The 6" (15cm) square should be in the middle when the project is hung.

- Plug-in style night-light with removable shade cover
- Assorted E beads, seed beads and micro beads
- Flat glass beads
- Brass charms and coins
- Glass adhesive
- Dimensional adhesive
- Shallow tray (optional)
- Heat gun

Project by Barbara Matthiessen

Night-lights can sparkle twenty-four hours a day with the simple addition of glass beads. You can whip one of these up for everyone you know in an afternoon. Then sit back and watch them glow!

SPARKLE NIGHT-LIGHT

TIP

If you work on both sides of the shade at once, you might have beads falling off the shade before the adhesive dries. Work over a shallow tray to reuse beads that fall from the night-light.

1 Remove the shade from the night-light.

2 Glue large glass beads on the shade using glass adhesive. Let the adhesive dry.

3 Apply dimensional adhesive to one side of the shade, then add the larger elements such as charms, glass beads or coins. Apply more dimensional adhesive and sprinkle E or seed beads over the surface.

4 Run the heat gun over the beaded surface just long enough to adhere the beads to the surface. The dimensional adhesive will still be tacky, but should hold the beads in place.

5 Repeat steps 3 and 4 for the other side of shade.

6 Add more drops of dimensional adhesive then sprinkle on micro beads to fill in areas that seem empty. Heat the adhesive with a heat gun. Repeat until the surface of the shade is covered with beads.

7 Allow adhesives to dry before the shade on the night-light. Glue the shade to the night-light with glass adhesive.

G I F T   C A R D S
A N D   P A C K A G E S

There is the presentation, and with a little crafting and planning, the packaging can be just as beautiful as the gift itself. Yours will be the gift that elicits smiles and gasps of pleasant surprise. Gift presentation such as this doesn't require a wallet full of money or a painful amount of time and effort. All you need is a little bit of crafting know-how and some creativity.

This section is filled with ideas to kick start the creativity, and enough step-by-step know-how to get you going. You'll find a card shaped like a dress for the playful friends on your gift-giving list. There is an elegant card featuring a Chinese coin. You could create a box featuring a surprise happy birthday banner. How would you like to make a decorative Chinese take-out box that is perfect for little gifts like jewelry? Or how about spicing up a gift of bath supplies with a gorgeous glass bottle and an elegant tag? There's something here for everyone.

Gather your pens and paper, clear off the table for crafting and don't let an opportunity for creative gift presentation go to waste.

This miniature mannequin model isn't just a fashion statement. Beneath the frilly skirt is a message from you. Create this couture card with a friendly note to celebrate a special occasion or as an invitation to a girls-only event. Once the occasion is over, the card makes a beautiful keepsake of the festivities!

DRESS UP CARD

MATERIALS

- ♥ White cardstock
- ♥ 44" (112cm) of ⅛" (3mm) wide white ribbon
- ♥ 12" × 5" (30cm × 13cm) of pink tulle
- ♥ 2' (61cm) of 18-gauge pink coated wire
- ♥ 6" (15cm) of 22-gauge pink coated wire
- ♥ Wire cutter
- ♥ Scissors
- ♥ Round-nose pliers
- ♥ Tape

1 To create the stand, loop the 18-gauge wire once around a pencil, leavine a 2" (5cm) tail on the shorter end of the wire.

2 Twist the shorter end of the wire two to three times around itself to seal the small loop, and then trim off the end. Beneath the looped area, bend the wire at a right angle. About 5" (13cm) from the loop, bend the wire at another right angle.

3 Create a flat spiral for the base. Just below the right angle you last made, use round-nose pliers to create a circle with four or five successively wider layers. When finished, curl the end with the round-nose pliers to form another, smaller spiral. Make sure the spirals are flat and the wire stands upright.

4 To create the smaller hanger, bend the 22-gauge wire at a right angle 2" (5cm) from one end. Bend again in the same direction 1¼" (3cm) further along the wire from the first bend. This will be the horizontal part of the hanger.

5 Bend the wire back toward the neck of the hanger, creating a right-hand bend. Twist the wire around the neck to secure, then trim the excess. Create a loop and spiral with the other end of the wire.

6 To create the dress, fold the white cardstock in half and place the top of the dress pattern, found on page 90, against the fold. Cut out the pattern from the folded piece of cardstock. Cut two slits in the fold (for the straps) where indicated on the pattern.

7 Cut two 2" (5cm) pieces of ribbon. Fold each in half and insert them in the slits to extend ⅜" (9mm) above the fold. Tape the ends inside the folded dress.

8 Fold the tulle lengthwise in half, and then in half again, so it is approximately 3" × 5" (8cm × 13cm). Lay the tulle over the waist of the card.

9 Tie a 36" (91cm) piece of ribbon around the tulle and card at the waist of the dress. Keep the knot at the back of the card and gather the tulle in the front so it resembles a skirt. Wrap the rest of the ribbon around the top (the bodice) of the dress. Tape the ribbon to itself in the back to secure.

10 Open the cardstock and write a message inside the dress. Then place the dress on the hanger and the hanger on the stand.

MORE IDEAS

- ■ Further embellish the dress with sequins and beads.
- ■ Use a mailing tube to send the finished card.
- ■ Personalize the wire or tulle with the colors of bridesmaid dresses or seasonal hues.

Project by Debba Haupert

- ♥ 4¼" × 11" (11cm × 28cm) piece of cardstock
- ♥ Decorative paper (or decorate a paper with rubber stamps)
- ♥ 9" (23cm) of ¼" (6mm) wide coordinating ribbon
- ♥ Costume jewel
- ♥ Hook and loop fastener
- ♥ Glue stick
- ♥ Craft glue
- ♥ ⅛" (3mm) hole punch
- ♥ Bone folder (or similar scoring tool)
- ♥ Ruler

Project by Drenda Barker

This card is perfect for birthdays, showers or just for fun. Include the party information to turn it into an invitation, or attach a small vellum envelope inside to include something special.

PURSE CARD

1 Use the glue stick to adhere the decorative paper to one side of the cardstock.

2 Use the pattern on page 90 to cut out the purse card from the cardstock.

3 Score and fold on the lines shown on the pattern. All folds should be made so the decorative paper is on the outside.

4 To attach the ribbon handle, make a ½" (13mm) mark from the left and right sides of the top fold. Use a ⅛" (3mm) hole punch to make a hole on each mark, and thread a ribbon through the holes. Tie a knot inside the fold to secure the ends.

5 Attach the hook and loop fastener inside the top fold of the card. Remove the backing from the other side of the fastener and press it in place against the card.

6 Attach a jewel to the front of the card with craft glue.

TIP

Place both halves of the hook and loop fastener together, remove the backing from one side and press it into place. Then remove the backing from the other side and press the cover of the card together. This assures proper placement of the fastener.

Project by *Drenda Barker*

Make a batch of these cards ahead of time, and keep them on hand for those last-minute gifts. Vary the color of the cardstock to make this card appropriate for birthdays, graduations and even weddings.

MONEY FRAME CARD

MATERIALS

♥ 8½" × 5½" (22cm × 14cm) piece of pine green cardstock

♥ 2½" × 3" (6cm × 8cm) piece of pine green cardstock

♥ 4" × 5¼" (10cm × 13cm) piece of dark green cardstock

♥ 2³⁄₈" × 2⁵⁄₈" (6cm × 7cm) piece of acetate

♥ Rubber stamp with script words

♥ Dollar bill

♥ Gold inkpad

♥ Gold thread

♥ Gold paint pen

♥ Brass mini brad

♥ Two brass eyelets with setting tools

♥ ⅛" (.3cm) hole punch

♥ Double stick tape

♥ Craft knife

♥ Cutting mat

1 Fold 8½" × 5½" (22cm × 14cm) cardstock in half so you have a card that is 4¼" × 5½" (11cm × 14cm).

2 Prepare the dark green cardstock by stamping lightly the script words using the gold inkpad and running a line of gold ink along the edges of card. Use the ⅛" (3mm) hole punch to punch a hole ⅛" (3mm) down from the top center of the card.

3 Cut out a 1³⁄₈" (3cm) square from the center of the 2½" × 3" (6cm × 8cm) cardstock. Use your paint pen to draw a decorative line around the cutout center. This will be the frame for the money.

4 Attach the acetate to the back of this cardstock frame with double stick tape.

5 Attach the two brass eyelets to the top corners of the cardstock frame.

6 Cut a 2½" (6cm) piece of double stick tape in half lengthwise, and place these strips along the right and left edges of the back of the cardstock frame. Place another uncut strip of double stick tape at the bottom of the frame. This should keep the face of the bill from slipping in the frame. Secure the cardstock frame to the front of the dark green cardstock using double stick tape.

7 Place gold thread through the eyelets on the frame so that both ends of thread come out through the front of the card. Put these ends through the hole at the top of the dark green cardstock. Tape the ends of the string to the back of the cardstock. Insert a brad through the same hole and secure the brad to the cardstock.

8 Use double stick tape to attach the entire cardstock frame to the card you prepared in step 1.

9 Insert a bill, with the face showing through the acetate, in the top of the frame.

Happy Birthday

Happy Birthday

Tiny hole-less beads and origami mesh are fabulous embellishments for cards. These are the kinds of card that will have people wondering how you did it.

BIRTHDAY CARDS

Butterfly Card

MATERIALS

- ♥ 8½" × 5½" (22cm × 14cm) piece of cardstock
- ♥ 2½" × 2¼" (6cm × 6cm) piece of decorative paper
- ♥ 2¼" × 2" (6cm × 5cm) piece of shiny black cardstock
- ♥ Butterfly paper punch
- ♥ Gold beads without holes
- ♥ 1½" × 1" (4cm × 3cm) piece of double-sided adhesive
- ♥ Glue stick or double stick tape

1 Fold the cardstock in half to create a card 4¼" × 5½" (11cm × 14cm).

2 Punch the butterfly shape in the center of a shiny piece of black cardstock.

3 Remove one side of the protective backing of a piece of double-sided adhesive, and place it on the back of the black cardstock. It should be directly over the punched butterfly shape, so the adhesive is exposed through the punched butterfly shape.

4 Sprinkle tiny gold beads over the adhesive on the front of the card, covering the butterfly shape with beads.

5 Remove protective backing from the other side of the adhesive and place the black

cardstock in the center of the decorative paper, with the beaded butterfly facing out.

6 Use a glue stick or double stick tape to adhere the decorative paper to the front of the card. Add text to the front of the card below the decorative paper.

Mesh Star Card

MATERIALS

- ♥ 8½" × 5½" (22cm × 14cm) piece of ivory cardstock
- ♥ 3⅛" × 2⅜" (8cm × 6cm) piece of ivory cardstock
- ♥ 1⅜" × 1½" (3cm × 4cm) piece of dark colored cardstock
- ♥ 3" × 2¼" (8cm × 8cm) piece of origami mesh paper
- ♥ Small piece of paper with the words "Happy Birthday"
- ♥ Star shape rubber stamp
- ♥ Clear embossing inkpad
- ♥ Four 2" (5cm) pieces of 28-gauge wire
- ♥ Two mini brads
- ♥ ⅛" (3mm) hole punch
- ♥ Push pin
- ♥ Craft knife
- ♥ Cutting mat
- ♥ Glue stick

1 Fold the 8½" × 5½" (22cm × 14cm) cardstock in half to create a card 4¼" × 5½" (11cm × 14cm). Use the star rubber stamp and an embossing inkpad to stamp star shapes randomly on the front of the card. This will be a very subtle effect.

2 Trace a star shape, using the template on page 91, in the center of the dark colored cardstock. Use a craft knife to carefully cut out the star shape from the dark colored paper. Glue the paper with the star-shaped hole ½" (13mm) from the top of the smaller piece of ivory cardstock.

3 Lay origami mesh paper over the smaller piece of ivory cardstock.

4 To adhere the mesh, use a pushpin to make two tiny holes through the mesh and the dark colored cardstock in each of the four corners.

5 Fold a piece of wire in half and insert it through the two holes at each corner. Secure the wire on the back of the smaller ivory cardstock.

6 Glue "Happy Birthday" on the mesh paper below the star shape. Punch a hole on each side of "Happy Birthday" and insert the mini brads.

7 Glue the smaller ivory cardstock to the larger card.

More great embellishments are used in these cards: coin envelopes—found at office supply stores— and a Chinese coin.

Star Envelope Card

MATERIALS

- ♥ 8½" × 5½" (22cm × 14cm) piece of cardstock
- ♥ 2½" × 4" (6cm × 10cm) piece of decorative paper
- ♥ 2¼" × 3½" (8cm × 9cm) coin envelope
- ♥ 1¾" × 2¾" (4cm × 7cm) cardstock tag
- ♥ Handmade paper for the star shape
- ♥ Brown and gold paint
- ♥ 8" (20cm) length of gold thread
- ♥ Metallic marker
- ♥ ⅛" (3mm) hole punch
- ♥ Three eyelets with setting tools
- ♥ Old toothbrush
- ♥ Scissors
- ♥ Glue stick
- ♥ Wax paper

1 Fold the cardstock in half to form a card 4¼" × 5½" (11cm × 14cm). Glue the decorative paper at an angle across the front of the card.

2 Use brown paint and an old toothbrush to make splatter marks on the card and decorative paper. To do this, dip the toothbrush into paint and run your thumb along the bristles of the brush.

3 Cut a small star shape, using the template on page 91, from the handmade paper. Attach the star shape to the flap of the coin envelope with an eyelet. Attach another eyelet to the bottom of the envelope.

4 Dip a small piece of crumpled wax paper into gold paint and dab it onto the back of the coin envelope. Use a metallic marker to draw squiggly lines down the back of the coin envelope.

5 Use the glue stick to adhere the front of the coin envelope at an angle on top of the decorative paper.

6 Punch a hole in the top of the tag and set an eyelet in it. Place gold thread through the eyelet and secure it to the tag. Place the tag into the envelope. Let the thread hang out of the envelope.

Chinese Coin Card

MATERIALS

- ♥ 8½" × 5½" (22cm × 14cm) piece of cardstock
- ♥ 2" × 2¼" (5cm × 8cm) piece of textured decorative paper
- ♥ ¾" × 3" (19mm × 8cm) piece of decorative paper
- ♥ Chinese coin
- ♥ Brown decorative chalk
- ♥ Two 2" (5cm) lengths of 24-gauge wire
- ♥ Two eyelets with setting tools
- ♥ Foam tape
- ♥ Double stick tape
- ♥ Glue stick

1 Fold the cardstock in half to form a card 4¼" × 5½" (11cm × 14cm).

2 Use the glue stick to attach the long thin piece of decorative paper to the shorter, wider piece of textured paper.

3 Set the eyelets into the sides of the wider piece of decorative paper. The eyelets should be approximately ⅛" (3mm) from the right and left edges of the paper.

4 Fold the wire in half and thread it through the hole in the center of the coin. Pull the wire end out from the coin center and twist them closed so there is a loop holding the wire to the coin.

5 Push the twisted ends of the wire through one of the eyelets in the decorative paper. Bend the excess wire over and attach it to the back of the paper with double stick tape. Repeat steps 4 and 5 on the other side of the coin with another piece of wire.

6 Use foam tape to adhere the decorative paper with coin embellishment to the front of the cardstock.

7 Rub a coordinated color of decorative chalk around the edges of the card. Use your fingers to blend the chalk for a more subtle effect.

Project by *Drenda Barker*

Matchbox

♥ Matchbox

♥ 2¹/₁₆" × 4¹/₈" (5cm × 10cm) piece of decorative paper

♥ 8" (20cm) coordinating ribbon

♥ Clear, flat glass marble

♥ Small piece of paper with printed words

♥ ¹/₈" (3mm) hole punch

♥ Brad (regular size)

♥ Awl

♥ Scissors

♥ E6000

♥ Dimensional adhesive

Accordion Book

♥ Two 1¹/₈" × 1³/₄" (3cm × 4cm) pieces of posterboard

♥ Two 1¹/₂" × 2¹/₈" (4cm × 5cm) pieces of decorative paper

♥ 8¹/₂" × 1⁵/₈" (22cm × 4cm) strip of bond paper

♥ Glue stick

This is a different kind of greeting that uses a matchbox and an accordion fold booklet to store your message. This card is sure to elicit gasps of delight and surprise.

MATCHBOX CARD

TO MAKE THE MATCHBOX

1 Place a small amount of dimensional adhesive over the printed words, then immediately place a marble over the glue. Let the glue dry. After the glue has dried completely, cut around the bottom of the marble and discard the extra paper.

2 Use E6000 to cover the outside of the matchbox with decorative paper.

3 Punch a ¹/₈" (3mm) hole in the middle of one of the short sides of the matchbox drawers. Make sure not to rip the matchbox.

4 To attach the ribbon to the drawer, use the awl to make a hole in the center of the length of ribbon, and push the brad through the ribbon. Push the brad through the hole in the drawer. Open the brad inside the box. The ribbon should now be secure. Tie a knot at the end of the ribbon.

5 Attach the glass marble with E6000 to the top of the matchbox.

TO MAKE THE ACCORDION BOOK

1 Use a glue stick to cover the posterboard with decorative paper. Miter the corners and trim off any excess paper.

2 (See the illustration below.) Fold the bond paper strip into 1" (3cm) pleats. Cut off the incomplete pleat at the end. Fold the paper back and forth to make an accordion.

3 Glue one posterboard cover to front of first pleat and one to the back of the last pleat. Add a message to the book and insert the book into the matchbox.

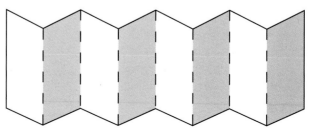

- 8½" × 11" (22cm × 28cm) sheet of dark blue pearlescent paper

- Small scraps of earth tone cardstock: pumpkin, sage, mustard and wine

- 12" (30cm) length of heavy silver tapestry braid

- Alphabet eyelets to spell "gift" or a word of your choice

- ⅛" (3mm) hole punch

- ¾" (19mm) circle paper punch

- Eyelet setter and hammer

- Bone folder

- Scissors

- Craft glue

Project by *Mary Lynn Maloney*

Make the box as thoughtful as the gift! It doesn't take long to create this clever little pouch that says "you're special." The pillow box template is all it takes to get started. Then embellish as shown, or take off in your own decorating direction.

PILLOW GIFT BOX

1 Transfer the pillow box template from page 91 onto the sheet of dark blue paper, making sure to indicate the fold lines. Cut the pillow box shape from the blue paper and score the fold lines with a bone folder.

2 Punch a ¾" (19mm) circle from each piece of the earth tone cardstock. Punch a tiny hole in the center of each circle using the ⅛" (3mm) hole punch. Insert the letter "g" eyelet into one tiny hole and set it with the eyelet setter and hammer. Repeat with the remaining cardstock circles and eyelet letters, spelling out the word "gift."

3 Lay the flat pillow box with the glue flap at the top edge. Position the length of silver braid approximately 1¼" (3cm) from bottom edge of pillow box. Use craft glue to adhere the assembled eyelet letters onto the pillow box and over the silver braid, spelling out the word "gift."

4 Tie knots in the loose ends of the silver braid and trim the excess braid. Unravel the ends of braid slightly. Let the glue dry.

5 Fold and assemble the pillow box, gluing the flap to the inside of the pouch. Fold in one end of the box, then insert a small gift before closing the other end.

MATERIALS

♥ 8½" × 11" (22cm × 28cm) sheet off-white 90# cold-press watercolor paper

♥ 4½" × 7" (11cm × 18cm) cellophane envelope with self-adhesive flap

♥ 8½" x 11" (22cm × 28cm) sheet of purple cardstock

♥ Pigment inks: Parchment, Topaz, Celadon and Eggplant (Colorbox)

♥ Celtic knotwork brass stencil (Dreamweaver Stencils)

♥ 4½" (11cm) length beaded fringe: purple, amber, blue

♥ Low-tack masking tape

♥ Fabric glue

♥ Two brass paper fasteners

♥ Stylus tool

♥ Gift card

♥ Bone folder

♥ Craft knife

♥ Scissors

♥ Light table (optional)

Project by *Mary Lynn Maloney*

Gift cards are everywhere these days, but their packaging can be a bit on the dull side. Add a little interest and pizazz to the gift card with this snappy fringed packet.

FRINGE BENEFITS CARD

1 Tear along one of the short edges of the watercolor paper, and then trim the watercolor paper to 4⅞" × 4" (12cm × 10cm), leaving the torn edge on one of the 4⅞" (12cm) sides.

2 Tape the Celtic stencil to the light table, or use a surface which allows you to see through the watercolor paper. Place the watercolor paper over the stencil and use a stylus to emboss the image onto the paper. Move the paper around several times and create a random embossing over the paper surface.

3 Remove the paper from the light table. With the raised image side up, lightly tap and swirl pigment inks across the embossed paper, beginning with the light colors. Don't use too much ink, and continue random, light applications of ink. Cover the entire paper, and let the ink dry.

4 Score and fold the embossed paper in half so that the torn edge is at the bottom. Use fabric glue to adhere the length of beaded fringe to the inside of the torn edge of embossed paper, with the beads hanging out. Let the glue dry.

5 Tear a sheet of purple cardstock so it is approximately 4¼" × 5½" (11cm × 14cm). Slip the torn paper into a cellophane envelope. Put a gift card into the envelope on top of the purple cardstock and seal the envelope.

6 Place the folded, embossed paper over the cellophane envelope. Use a craft knife to make two small slits through the assembled packet and insert brass paper fasteners through the slits. Open the prongs in the back to secure.

You will come into some unexpected spending money.

Project by Drenda Barker

MATERIALS

- ♥ 4" (10cm) square piece of textured handmade paper
- ♥ 4" (10cm) square piece of bond paper
- ♥ Dollar bill
- ♥ Written fortune
- ♥ Glue stick
- ♥ Scissors
- ♥ Compass or a circle cutter

Everyone loves fortune cookies. Make them fun, but not edible, by adding currency and creating your own personalized fortunes. It's a perfect fit in a nesting box.

MONEY FORTUNE COOKIE

1 Create a fortune and write it or print it out.

2 Use the glue stick to attach the bond paper to the handmade paper.

3 Cut out a 3¾" (10cm) circle from the paper using the circle cutter or the compass. Fold the circle in half and make a small pinch mark in the center of the circle. Do not fold the circle completely along this line.

4 Fold the money in thirds lengthwise, and then in half. Place the money in the center of circle, so it lies in the opposite direction of the pinch you just made.

5 Bring the edge of the circle together along the pinch fold and glue the edges together. You should have something that looks like a tube.

6 Fold the tube in half at the pinch mark you made in step 3. Do not fold the ends of the cookie, only the center of the tube.

7 Place a small piece of glue in the center of the fold. This will hold the cookie together.

8 Glue the fortune on top of the cookie with the money folded inside the cookie.

MORE IDEAS

Find an inspirational saying or some good wishes and use it as your fortune. Or write the fortune on the paper cookie itself. Keep a journal of good sayings so you never need to search for a creative fortune.

Project by *Mary Lynn Maloney*

MATERIALS

- ♥ Wrapped bar of soap
- ♥ 5" × 7" (13cm × 18cm) sheet of purple mulberry paper
- ♥ Two glass bottles with cork stoppers
- ♥ Three 1⅞" × 3¾" (5cm × 10cm) manila shipping tags
- ♥ Pigment inkpads: Seaglass, Celadon, Topaz (ColorBox)
- ♥ Three yards (3m) of assorted textured fibers: green/gold, purple/blue
- ♥ Fifteen assorted glass beads
- ♥ Vintage alphabet set
- ♥ Three silver eyelet frames
- ♥ Eight brass ⅛" (3mm) eyelets with setting tools
- ♥ ⅛" (3mm) hole punch
- ♥ Scissors
- ♥ Glue stick

Give the gift of calm (calme), luxury (luxe) and beauty (jolie) with a set of pampering bath products adorned with fun, funky hang tags.

EMBELLISHED BOTTLES

1 Tear the purple mulberry paper to fit and wrap around the bar of soap, leaving approximately ½" (13mm) of soap showing at either end. Glue the mulberry paper to the bottom of the soap.

2 Randomly tap and swirl the Seaglass, Celadon and Topaz inkpads onto the three manila tags. Let the ink dry.

3 Place an eyelet frame on each manila tag. Cut out the alphabet letters to spell out the French words "calme," "jolie" and "luxe." Using the eyelet frames as guides, arrange the words to fit within the frames and glue the words onto the tags.

4 Make a pencil mark on the tags through each eyelet hole. Punch the tags where pencil marks indicate. Insert the eyelets into punched holes and attach the eyelet frames to tags with the setting tool and hammer.

5 Loop the textured fibers through each tag opening, trimming the fibers to the desired length. Thread beads onto the dangling fibers. Knot the fibers around the necks of the bottles and around the soap. Add more beads to any dangling fibers as desired.

TIP

Some of the eyelet frames in the package have no eyelet holes. If you choose to use these frames, simply glue them onto the tag with craft glue, as was done with the tag on the soap.

Project by *Barbara Matthiessen*

These sachets are quick and easy to make, perfect for a bridal shower or as a sweet surprise in a gift basket. Use soft, herbal fragrances or try adding essential oils, like vanilla or lavender, to potpourri.

VELLUM SACHETS

1 Use white ink to stamp a background in the center of the vellum. Keep the stamp 1" (3cm) away from the top of the vellum. This project assumes the background stamp you choose is 4" × 5" (10cm × 13cm).

2 Turn stamped image face down. Fold both long sides in towards the center making a crease across the sheet. Stop your fold at the edge of the stamped image. The sides will not meet in the center. Unfold, and then fold the short sides into the center. They will overlap by ½" (13mm). Unfold.

3 Use scissors to trim the corner sections where the long side and short side folds overlap. Cut to the long side fold along the short side fold line. Repeat this step on all four corners.

4 Refold the vellum. Tape the short sides together in the center with double stick tape. Place potpourri or herbs inside the vellum pocket then fold the long sides in.

5 Tie a ribbon around the vellum. Place the center of a 24" (61cm) ribbon on the center of the front. Wrap it around to the back and cross the ends of the ribbon. Bring the ribbon around in opposite directions to the front then tie a knot or bow. Add beads, charms or herbs to the knot.

MORE IDEAS

■ Sachets such as this can be tiny gift wraps of any size.

■ Place folded money or gift certificates inside or try candies in the bundles.

Wrapping gifts does not have to be boring! Try this unusual way to present your next gift. Fashioned after a Chinese food take-out box, it takes gift presentation to a completely new level.

CHINESE TAKE-OUT BOX

MATERIALS

- ♥ 8½" (22cm) square piece of cardstock
- ♥ 5" (13cm) square piece of cardstock
- ♥ ³⁄₈" (9mm) wide and 18" (46cm) long piece of ribbon
- ♥ Pony bead
- ♥ Double stick tape
- ♥ Bone folder
- ♥ Ruler
- ♥ Awl
- ♥ Scissors

TO MAKE THE BOX

1 Score and fold the 8½" (22cm) square cardstock in half and then unfold. Rotate the paper one quarter turn, and then score and fold cardstock in half again. You should have two crossed lines on the cardstock.

2 With a corner of the cardstock facing you, bring the bottom point up to the top point and fold the cardstock in half. Rotate the paper one quarter turn, then score and fold the cardstock in half again. You should now have four crossed lines, and the cardstock should be divided into eight parts.

3 Fold the cardstock in half to make a triangle with the points at the top. Hold this shape in your left hand, with your thumb just on the vertical line in the center of the triangle. With your right hand, push up on the bottom right edge of the triangle, close to the point. Turn the triangle slightly, so you can get a side view. If you fold on the previously made fold lines, you should see a square. Press on the line in the center of this square and crease well. You should now have two points on the right. Repeat this process on the left side of the triangle.

4 Place the cardstock with the point facing you and the opening at the top. From the bottom point, measure 1½"(4cm) up both the left and right sides of the triangle. Score and fold a straight line from the marks that you just made. Unfold this line.

5 Take the right point on the top layer and bring it to the middle fold line. Fold and crease well, keeping the line you just made in step 4 perpendicular before you. Repeat this step on the left side, bringing the left point on the top layer to the middle fold line. Unfold both the left and right points. Turn the project over and repeat this step.

6 Take the point at the top of the project and fold down and create a triangle. Fold and crease well. Unfold. Repeat for the opposite point.

7 Open the cardstock completely. You should see a square in the very center of the cardstock. This will be the bottom of your box.

8 Fold the cardstock on the score marks so that the sides of the box are formed. As you are shaping, the triangles on the ends of the sides should be folded against the sides of the box so that you have overlapping triangles on two opposite sides of the box. Use double stick tape to secure the points of these triangles.

9 Fold the triangles above the top of the box (on sides that do not have overlapping triangles) inside the box and secure the points with double stick tape.

10 To secure the ribbon, make holes in the sides of the box that have the triangles folded on the outside. The holes should be made at the tip of the upside down triangle. Thread the ribbon through the holes and knot the ribbon on the inside of box.

TO MAKE THE LID

1 Score and fold ¾" (19mm) along each edge of the 5" (13cm) square cardstock. The folds should make a square in the corners of the lid.

2 Make ¾" (19mm) cuts on the left and right sides of the lid, along the inside folds of the squares in the corner. This will be a total of four cuts.

3 With the top of the lid facing down, fold the sides up and tuck the edges from the longer sides inside the lid.

4 Apply double stick tape on the inside of both of the short sides of the lid and secure them to the outside of the other edges. Place the lid on the box, and then thread a pony bead through the top of the ribbon handle.

Every time they pull off the lid to this box, it will make them smile.
What a great way to say "Happy Birthday," without spending a
lot of money.

HAPPY BIRTHDAY BOX

MATERIALS

- ♥ 2½" × 2½" × 1¾" (6cm × 6cm × 4cm) box with a lid
- ♥ Four pieces of 2" × 1" (5cm × 3cm) color coordinated cardstock
- ♥ Written words "Happy Birthday to You" printed on vellum or colored cardstock
- ♥ 10" (25cm) length of 1" (3cm) wide ribbon
- ♥ Five 4³⁄₈" (11cm) jump rings
- ♥ 1¼" (3cm) jump ring
- ♥ ¼" (6mm) eyelet with setting tool
- ♥ Eight ⅛" (3mm) eyelets with setting tools
- ♥ Bead on pin
- ♥ ⅛" (3mm) hole punch
- ♥ ³⁄₁₆" (5mm) anywhere hole punch
- ♥ Ruler
- ♥ Craft glue

1 Use a ruler to make small diagonal lines from each corner of the box lid to find the center of the box top. Use the anywhere hole punch to punch a hole in the center of the lid. Insert and set a ¼" (6mm) eyelet through this hole.

2 Print each word on two different colored cardstock pieces. Make sure the colors of the cardstock coordinate with the color of your box. Trim the cardstock pieces so they measures 2" × 1" (5cm × 3cm) and then glue the pieces of cardstock with the same word together.

3 Use the ⅛" (.3cm) hole punch to punch holes in the center of the top and bottom of each word. Insert and set the ⅛" (.3cm) eyelets in the holes.

4 Beginning with the top of *Happy*, attach the larger jump rings to secure the words together, making sure you attach words so that the colors alternate. Make a line of words.

5 Use the smallest jump ring to attach a bead on a pin to the bottom of the banner you just made.

6 Fold the ribbon in half and insert both ends through the jump ring at the top of

Happy. Fold the edge of the ribbon to a point and place craft glue over the point. Fold the point up onto the ribbon, securing it to the jump ring.

7 Insert the top of the ribbon through the bottom of the box lid. Leave about ½" (13mm) of ribbon hanging from the eyelet, which will leave enough room so that the words can easily be seen from the bottom of the lid. Knot the ribbon on the top of the box and tie a bow.

MORE IDEAS

Use the box as a gift presentation, and change the words on the banner to match the theme of the gift. This would make an excellent graduation gift presentation with an inspirational note on the banner. You can make this project with almost any size box. Just adjust the measurements to fit the box you are using.

This is a great way to organize tags that you've made, using paper and ribbon scraps, and makes a fantastic gift for any crafty friends you know who would love to share and swap tag art.

TAG BOX

MATERIALS

Box

- ♥ 11" (28cm) square piece of posterboard
- ♥ Four pieces of $2^{7}/_{8}$" × $3^{7}/_{8}$" (7cm × 10cm) posterboard for the sides
- ♥ $2^{7}/_{8}$" × $2^{7}/_{8}$" (7cm × 7cm) piece of posterboard for the bottom
- ♥ $5^{1}/_{4}$" (13cm) square piece of posterboard for the lid
- ♥ Four pieces of $3^{1}/_{2}$" × $4^{1}/_{2}$" (9cm × 11cm) decorative paper for the sides
- ♥ $3^{1}/_{2}$" (9cm) square piece of decorative paper for the bottom
- ♥ $5^{1}/_{2}$" (14cm) square piece of decorative paper for the lid
- ♥ Four 4" (10cm) pieces of elastic cord or clear elastic
- ♥ Glue stick
- ♥ Double stick tape
- ♥ Ruler
- ♥ Bone folder or other scoring tool
- ♥ Scissors

Tags

- ♥ Twelve 2" × $3^{3}/_{8}$" (5cm × 9cm) scraps of cardstock
- ♥ Twelve pieces scrap decorative paper to cover cardstock
- ♥ $1/_{8}$" (3mm) hole punch
- ♥ Twelve $1/_{8}$" (3mm) eyelets and setting tools
- ♥ Ribbon
- ♥ Glue stick

TO MAKE THE BOX

1 Cover the four side pieces of posterboard for the inside of box, and the one piece of posterboard that will be the inside bottom of the box, with decorative paper. Set these aside

2 Draw a line 4" (10cm) from each side of the 11" (28cm) square piece of posterboard. You should have four lines that make a smaller box inside the square, and a 4" (10cm) box in each corner. Cut out all four corners.

3 Using your bone folder, or another scoring tool, score the pencil lines that outline the 3" (8cm) square in the center of the posterboard. Fold, crease and unfold the lines. You should now see the bottom and sides of the box taking shape.

4 On the inside of two opposite sides of the box place a small piece of double stick tape, 1" (3cm) from the top, on both the left and right edges of the side. Adhere the ends of the elastic to the tape and pull the elastic taut around the front. For the other two opposite sides, place a small amount of double stick tape $1^{1}/_{2}$" (4cm) from the top on both the left and right edges, adhere the ends of the elastic to this tape and pull the elastic taut around the front. You should have a piece of elastic secured around each of the four sides of the box.

5 Run a line of double stick tape around the edges on all four sides of the box, and press the decorative paper-covered posterboard piece into place on the double stick tape. Make sure not to cover the elastic. Press the other piece of posterboard covered in decorative paper on the inside bottom of the box. These pieces should cover all the double stick tape you used on the box.

TO MAKE THE LID

1 Cover $5^{1}/_{4}$" (13cm) posterboard with decorative paper. Cut off any excess paper.

2 Measure and score 1" (3cm) from each edge. Crease and then unfold. This creates a square in each corner. Make a single 1" (3cm) cut on the left and right sides of lid, along the inside folds of each square on those sides. This will be a total of four cuts.

3 With the top of the lid facing down, fold the sides up and tuck the edges from the longer sides inside the lid.

4 Apply double stick tape on the inside of both short sides of the lid and secure them to the outside of the other edges.

TO MAKE TAGS:

1 Use the pattern on page 91 to cut the tags from scrap cardstock.

2 Adhere the decorative paper scraps to the cardstock. Punch a $1/_{8}$" (3mm) hole in the center where indicated on the tags and set an eyelet in the hole.

3 Attach a ribbon through the hole in the tags. Secure the tags under the elastic on the inside panels of the box. Secure the box closed with the lid.

TEMPLATES

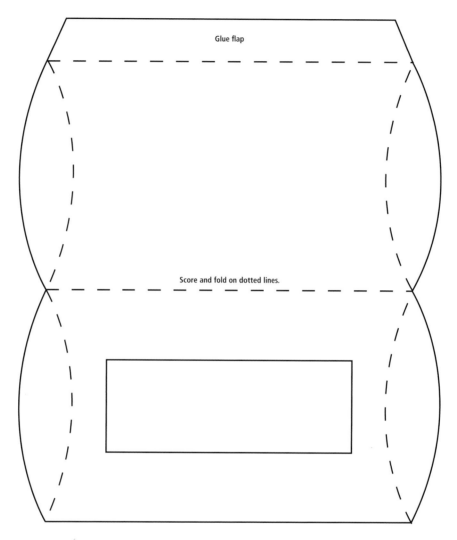

Glue flap

Score and fold on dotted lines.

MAGNETS IN A PILLOW BOX.
See page 20.

HEART PINS.
See page 33.

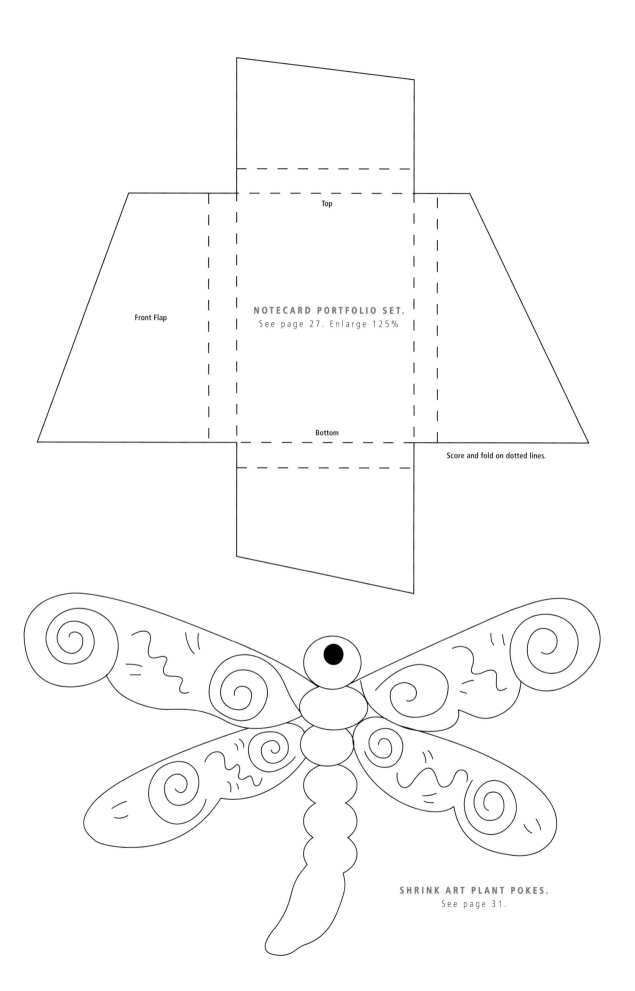

Top

Front Flap

NOTECARD PORTFOLIO SET.
See page 27. Enlarge 125%

Bottom

Score and fold on dotted lines.

SHRINK ART PLANT POKES.
See page 31.

SHRINK ART PLANT POKES.
See page 31.

PURSE CARD.
See page 70. Enlarge 118%.

Top

Fold

Fold

Bottom

Cut   Cut
Fold

DRESS UP CARD.
See page 69.

90

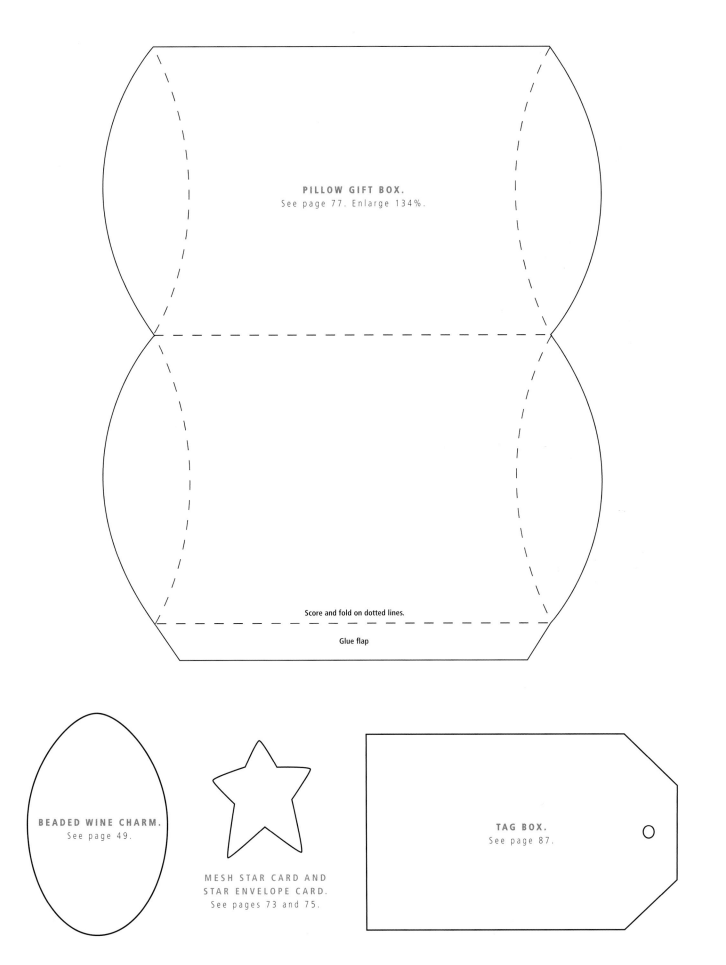

PILLOW GIFT BOX.
See page 77. Enlarge 134%.

Score and fold on dotted lines.

Glue flap

BEADED WINE CHARM.
See page 49.

**MESH STAR CARD AND
STAR ENVELOPE CARD.**
See pages 73 and 75.

TAG BOX.
See page 87.

RESOURCES

Most of the materials used in this book can be found at your local arts and crafts store. Another excellent resource can be the Internet. Included below are a list of some of the companies whose products were used in the projects. Good luck and happy crafting!

STAMPS AND INKS

A Stamp in the Hand Co.
20507 S. Belshaw Ave.
Carson, CA 90746
(310) 884-9700
fax: (310) 884-9888
www.astampinthehand.com

All Night Media
Plaid Enterprises
3225 West Tech Drive
Norcrest, GA 30092
(800) 842-4197
www.allnightmedia.com
Stamps, Colorbox and Ancient Page inks and Gallery Glass

Impression Obsession
P.O. Box 5415
Williamsburg, VA 23188
(877) 259-0905
www.impression-obsession.com
Stamps, cardstock and accessories

Postmodern Design
P.O. Box 26432
Oklahoma City, OK 73126-0432
(405) 826-0289
Fax: (405) 525-4112

Ranger Industries, Inc.
15 Park Road
Tinton Falls, NJ 07724
(800) 244-2211
Perfect Pearls, UTEE, pigment stamp pads, Posh Inkablities

Rubber Stampede
Delta Technical Coatings
2550 Pellissier Place
Whittier, CA 90601
(800) 632-8386
fax: (800) 546-6888
www.deltacrafts.com/RubberStampede
Stamps and paints

SonLight Impressions Stamps
Sierra Enterprises
P.O. Box 5325
Petaluma, CA 94955
(888) 765-6051
fax: (888) 765-6051
www.sierra-enterprises.com
Stamps and craft supplies

Stampers Anonymous
25967 Detroit Rd.
Westlake, OH 44145
(888) 326-0012
fax: (440) 250-9117
www.stampersanonymous.com

Tsukineko, Inc.
15411 NE 95th St.
Redmond, WA 98052
(800) 769-6633
www.tsukineko.com
Inks

Zettiology
39570 SE Park St. #201
Snoqualmie, WA 98065
(425) 888-3191
zettiologist@hotmail.com
www.thestudiozine.com

POLYMER CLAY

American Art Clay Co., Inc. (AMACO)
4717 W 16th Street
Indianapolis, IN 46222-2598
(800) 374-1600
Fax: (317) 248-9300
www.amaco.com
Fimo Classic, Fimo Soft, gold leaf, clay blades, molds tools and polymer clay accessories

Kato Polyclay
Van Aken International
P. O. Box 1680
Rancho Cucamonga, CA 91729
(909) 980-2001
Fax: (909) 980-2333
www.vanaken.com
Polymer clay, clay blades and acrylic rollers

Polyform Products Co.
1901 Estes Ave.
Elk Grove Village, IL 60007
(847) 427-0020
www.sculpey.com

GENERAL CRAFT SUPPLIES

Artistic Wire
1210 Harrison Ave.
La Grange Park, IL 60526
(630) 530-7567
Fax: (630) 530-7536
www.artisticwire.com
Wire and tools for crafting

Clearsnap
P.O. Box 98
Anacortes, WA 98221
(360) 293-6634
www.clearsnap.com
Stamps, inks and crafting supplies

Creative XPress!
295 W. Center St.
Provo, UT 84601
(800) 563-8679

Fax: (801) 373-1446
Craft materials and scrapbook supplies

Dreamweaver Stencils
www.dreamweaverstencils.com
Stencils

Duncan Enterprises
5673 E. Shields Ave.
Fresno, California 93727
(800) 237-2642
Fax: (559) 291-9444
www.duncanceramics.com
Ceramics, adhesives, paints and craft supplies

Fiskars Brands, Inc.
School, Office & Craft
7811 W. Stewart Avenue
Wausau, WI 54401 USA
(800) 500-4849
www.fiskars.com
consumeraffairs@fiskars.com
Crafting and paper crafting tools

JudiKins
17803 S. Harvard Blvd.
Gardena, CA 90248
(310) 515-1115
www.judikins.com
Stamps, adhesives and crafting supplies

Paper Adventures
P.O. Box 04393
Milwaukee, WI 53204-0393
(800) 727-0699
Fax: (800) 727-0268
www.paperadventures.com
Crafting cardstock and papers

Plaid Enterprises
3225 West Tech Drive
Norcrest, GA 30092
(800) 842-4197

www.plaidonline.com
Gallery glass and other crafting supplies

Provo Craft
151 E. 3450 North
Spanish Fork, UT 84660
(800) 937-7686
Fax: (801) 794-9001
www.provocraft.com
Crafting and paper crafting supplies

Ranger Ink
15 Park Rd.
Trinton Falls, NJ 07750
(800) 244-2211
Fax: (800) 266-1397
www.rangerink.com
Stamps, inks, paints and embossing supplies

Rupert, Gibbons & Spider
1147 Healdsburg Ave.
Healdsburg, CA 95448
(707) 433-9577
Fax: (707) 433-4906
www.jacquardproducts.com
Painting supplies and dyes

Speedball Art Products Co.
2226 Speedball Rd.
Statesville, NC 28677
(800) 898-7224
Fax: (704) 838-1472
Pens, inks, paints and watercolor

Walnut Hollow Farm, Inc.
1409 State Rd. 23
Dodgeville, WI 53533
(800) 950-5101
www.walnuthollow.com
Unfinished wood products and supplies for crafting and hobbyists

INDEX

A - C

Accordian-Fold CD Holder, 16, 17
All Keyed Up Box, 56, 57
baby gifts, 32, 46
Baby Memory Book Cover, 46
Beaded Wine Charms, 49, 91
beads, 30, 31, 33, 34, 36, 37, 41, 42, 44, 45, 49, 63, 64, 65
Bejeweled Photo Frame, 40
Birthday Cards, 73
Blooming Pens, 24
bookmarks, 35, 44
boxes
    All Keyed Up Box, 57
    Chinese Take-Out Box, 83
    Happy Birthday Box, 85
    Pillow Gift Box, 77
    Tag Box, 87
    Butterfly Card, 73
candles
    Heart Candle Snuffer, 37
    Metallic Candle, 36
    Mosaic Candleholder, 53
cardstock, 17, 20, 23, 27, 34, 44, 69, 70, 71, 73, 75, 78, 83, 85
CDs, 17, 60
Chinese Coin Card, 75
Chinese Take-Out Box, 82, 83
Collage Clock, 60
Collapsible Photo Album, 22, 23

D - F

decoupage, 21, 40, 59
Dogtag Domino Pendant, 45
Domino Photo Holder, 41
dominos, 41, 45
Dream Pillow, 61
Dress Up Card, 68, 69, 90
Embellished Bottles, 80
Embossed Bookmark, 35
embossing, 14, 33, 35, 36
eyelets, 18, 32, 71, 75, 77, 80, 85
Florentine Push Pin Set, 21
Flower Frame, 55

Flowerpots, Square, 54
flowers
    pressed, 18
    silk, 24, 55
foam board, 21, 25
frames, photo
Bejeweled Photo Frame, 40
Flower Frame, 55
Tri-Fold Mesh Frame, 32
French Bulletin Board, 58
Fringe Benefits Gift Card, 78

G - I

Garden Journal, 18
gardening gifts
    Flowerpots, Square, 54
    Garden Journal, 18
Shrink Art Plant Pokes, 31
gift cards
    Birthday Cards, 73
    Chinese Coin Card, 75
    Dress Up Card, 69
    Fringe Benefits Gift Card, 78
    Matchbox Card, 76
    Money Frame Card, 71
    Purse Card, 70
    Star Envelope Card, 75
gift packages
    Chinese Take-Out Box, 83
    Happy Birthday Box, 85
    Pillow Gift Box, 77
    Tag Box, 87
Happy Birthday Box, 84, 85
Heart Brooch, 43
Heart Candle Snuffer, 37
Heart Cork, 48
Heart Pins, 33, 88
Incense Burner Gift Set, 38, 39

J - L

Jacob's Ladder Stationery Set, 13
jewelry
    Dogtag Domino Pendant, 45
    Heart Brooch, 43

    Heart Pins, 33
    Mini Book Pendant, 15
    Prayer Box Necklace, 42
journals
    Garden Journal, 18
    Mini Book Pendant, 15
    Tag Journal, 14
lavender, 52, 61, 81
Lavender Banner, 52
Love Bookmark, 44

M - P

Magnets in a Pillow Box, 20, 88
Matchbox Card, 76
Mesh Star Card, 73, 91
Message in a Bottle, 34
Metallic Candle, 36
metric conversion chart, 4
Mini Book Pendant, 15
Money Fortune Cookie, 79
Money Frame Card, 71
Mosaic Candleholder, 53
Notecard Portfolio Set, 26, 27, 89
origami, 23
paper
    decorative, 13, 15, 17, 19, 21, 23, 25, 27, 39, 58, 70, 75, 76, 77, 87
    handmade, 21, 47, 79
    origami, 32
    watercolor, 27, 78
    wrapping, 40
Patterned Pencil Set, 19
photos
    Bejeweled Photo Frame, 40
    Collapsible Photo Album, 23
    Domino Photo Holder, 41
    Flower Frame, 55
    Tri-Fold Mesh Frame, 32
    Vintage Suitcase Photo Album, 47
Pillow Gift Box, 77, 91
Plaster Word Plaques, 30
polymer clay, 39, 43, 48, 53
Prayer Box Necklace, 42

Purse Card, 70, 90
Push Pin Holder, 25

R-W
rubber stamping, 14, 18, 27, 33, 34, 35, 41, 45, 54, 57, 71, 81
scented gifts
   Dream Pillow, 61
   Incense Burner Gift Set, 39
   Lavender Banner, 52
   Vellum Sachets, 81
scrapbooks, 18, 46
Shrink Art Plant Pokes, 31, 89, 90
shrink plastic, 31, 49
Sparkle Night-Light, 65
Star Envelope Card, 75, 91
stationery
   Jacob's Ladder Stationery Set, 13
   Notecard Portfolio Set, 27
Sun Catcher, 64
Tag Box, 86, 87, 91
Tag Journal, 14
tags, 14, 18, 57, 75, 80, 87
templates, 88–91
travel gifts
   Vintage Correspondence Tray, 59
   Vintage Suitcase Photo Album, 47
   Tri-Fold Mesh Frame, 32
   Vellum Sachets, 81
Vintage Correspondence Tray, 59
Vintage Suitcase Photo Album, 47
Wind Chime, 62, 63
wire, 15, 30, 31, 36, 37, 42, 49, 63, 69
writing tools
   Blooming Pens, 24
   Patterned Pencil Set, 19

Acetate: Any type of clear film or overhead transparency. Makes an excellent "window" for gift boxes.

Bond paper: Also known as text weight, plain or computer paper, this is any lightweight paper that you can easily use in a home computer printer.

Bone folder: A tool used to score paper and make sharp creases. Plastic pan scrapers or a paper clip inserted in the handle of a craft knife make excellent alternatives.

Cardstock: Also known as cover paper, this is a little heavier stock than bond paper and is usually what is used to make greeting cards.

Chipboard: This is a heavy cardboard used to make sturdy projects such as book and journal covers.

Craft glue: This is a glue that is thicker than white glue and can hold embellishments much better. Craft glue appears milky when wet and may not dry clear.

Decorative paper: Paper printed with a pattern or design, often themed for special occasions. Look for archival-quality paper for projects, as it will deteriorate less over time.

Dimensional adhesive: This is an adhesive that dries clear and is excellent for push pins and magnets. Diamond Glaze by Judikins and Dimensional Magic by Plaid are examples of dimensional adhesives.

E6000: This is the brand name of an industrial strength adhesive. It is also known as Goop. Use it for adding dimensional embellishments to projects.

Embossing powders: To use embossing powders, sprinkle the powder on wet ink or spread it over a project. Use a heat gun to melt the powder and create a raised design. It comes in a variety of colors.

Eyelet and eyelet setter: A small, typically metal ring used for a decorative effect in a project or to thread a cord. The setter is a small hammer.

Glue stick: A solid adhesive that dries quickly and cleanly. It is very useful for attaching papers together.

Handmade paper: This paper is usually softer and more fabric-like than machine-made paper. It may include plant matter for a more organic look.

Hook and loop fastener: A reuseable fastener such as Velcro.

Inks: There are three basic ink types: dye, pigment and solvent. Dye-based ink is water soluble. Pigment inks are used for embossing and archival applications. Solvent-based inks are used mainly for stamping on unusual surfaces such as plastic and ceramic.

Mitering: When covering an object, such as chipboard with decorative paper, mitering is used to make neat corners on the covering. First, make an angled cut from the corner of the paper to the corner of the object. Next, glue one side of the paper to the back of the object, and then the other. This will give you a crisp, clean corner.

Mounting tape: This is a high-density, double-sided foam tape that is useful for mounting pictures and papers in craft projects. It is an extremely strong adhesive.

Scoring: To score, mark your measurements for folding with the sharp end of a bone folder or another scoring tool. This will help eliminate cracks in the paper when you fold and keep the creases sharper.

Stylus: This is a tool for scoring and dry-embossing paper. It usually has a small metal ball on the end of a pen-shaped handle.

Vellum: A translucent paper which can give crafting projects a more elegant feel.

The best in creative craft instruction and inspiration is from
NORTH LIGHT BOOKS!

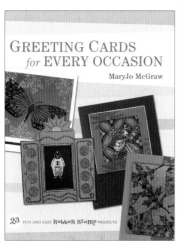

Renowed crafter MaryJo McGraw shares her most creative card ideas. With complete, step-by-step instructions and 23 detailed projects, it's easy to make your sentiments more personal and meaningful. You'll find a wealth of inspiring card ideas for nearly every holiday and occasion, including Christmas, Valentine's Day, Mother's and Father's Day, birthday, get well soon, new job and much more!

ISBN 1-58180-410-5, paperback, 128 pages, #32580-K

Inspired by the Garden presents 12 garden-inspired projects for inside and out. Using a range of crafting techniques and materials, this book showcases fun yet sophisticated garden décor projects perfect for crafters of all skill levels. Featuring popular garden motifs, projects include mosaic garden tables, matching pots and watering can, cards made with pressed flowers, a garden apron and more!

ISBN 1-58180-434-2, paperback, 128 pages, #32630-K

Let Tera Leigh act as your personal craft guide and motivator. She'll help you discover just how creative you really are. You'll explore eight exciting crafts through 16 fun, fabulous projects, including rubber stamping, bookmaking, papermaking, collage, decorative painting and more. Tera prefaces each new activity with insightful essays and encouraging advice.

ISBN 1-58180-293-5, paperback, 128 pages, #32170-K

Let Mary Jo McGraw, renowned rubber stamp artist and card maker, show you how to create handmade cards that capture the look and feel of antiques and heirlooms. You'll create 23 gorgeous cards using easy-to-find heirloom papers, old family photos and ephemera.

ISBN 1-58180-413-X, paperback, 128 pages, #32583-K

These and other fine North Light titles are available from your local art & craft retailer, bookstore, online supplier or by calling 1-800-448-0915.